33 DAYS TO
FREEDOM
FROM
LUST

A HOPE-FILLED DEVOTIONAL

33 DAYS TO
FREEDOM
FROM
LUST

DR. JARED MOORE

33 Days to Freedom From Lust: A Hope-Filled Devotional

Published by:

Coram Deo Media

Email: jared@drjaredmoore.com
Website: drjaredmoore.com

Cover design by Jerry Dorris at authorsupport.com

ISBN: 979-8-9937979-0-8

For additional Christian titles, please visit Jared's website at drjaredmoore.com

Are you shackled by sexual lust? Victory is possible—Jesus Christ can set you free! Unleashing the blazing light and beauty of the triune God in all His glorious attributes, Dr. Jared Moore exposes the darkness and ugliness of lust. With a helpful (and delightfully creative) method, he points the struggling soul to Scripture, poetry, and song—for when our souls are filled with the Spirit, with the Word of God, and with exuberant praise, the lasting pleasures of godliness become sweet and the shallow allurements of lust quickly lose their luster. If you are struggling with lust, this month of devotions—soaked in prayer and applied diligently to the heart—will provide an armory of spiritual weapons for the battle.

— Dr. Joel R. Beeke

Chancellor, Puritan Reformed Theological Seminary
Pastor, Heritage Reformed Congregation, Grand Rapids, MI

In *33 Days to Freedom from Lust*, Dr. Jared Moore confronts one of the great spiritual crises of the 21st century—lust—with biblical clarity and pastoral hope. At a time when rampant pornography use and other perversion is normalized and even celebrated, Moore reminds readers that Scripture calls it what it is: sin. Drawing from passages like Romans 8:13 and Colossians 3:5, he shows that lust is not an inevitable burden but a deadly habit that can be crucified through the power of the Holy Spirit. Each daily meditation turns the reader's focus from fleeting pleasure to the eternal beauty and holiness of God, helping Christians think God's thoughts after Him and cultivate a heart shaped by worship rather than desire. This book is both a sober warning and a gospel-saturated guide—calling believers to reject the lies of our porn-saturated culture and embrace the freedom and purity found only in Christ.

— Megan Basham

New York Times bestselling author, *Shepherds for Sale*
Journalist, *The Daily Wire*

Pastor Moore has written a faithful devotional for all defeated strugglers. Saturated in Scripture and pastoral care, *33 Days to Freedom From Lust* guides the struggler to become a victorious warrior against lust. Dr. Moore shows from Scripture that no Christian must live in bondage to sin.

— Dr. Rosaria Butterfield

Author, *Five Lies of our Anti-Christian Age*

Dr. Moore doesn't hand you clichés; he hands you a shovel. This book helps you dig out the roots of lust with the truth of Scripture and the power of the Spirit. It's plainspoken, biblical, and doable. If you're tired of making excuses and ready to get free, *33 Days to Freedom From Lust* will show you where to start and how to keep going.

— Michael Foster

Author, *It's Good to Be a Man*
Pastor, East River Church, Batavia, OH

In an era marked by the widespread rejection of Christian sexual ethics, both in the culture and sadly in the church too, *33 Days to Freedom From Lust* by Dr. Jared Moore stands out as a biblically faithful exception. This book is packed with both Scripture and practical guidance to empower Christians to put to death the lust of the flesh and live in purity and freedom before the Lord. This is no mere 'self-help' book, it is a powerful reminder that if the Son has set you free, you are and can be free indeed! Buy this book, read it, give it away, and stock it in your church's bookstall—you will be thankful that you did.

— **William Wolfe**

Executive Director, Center for Baptist Leadership

In a world that treats lust like an identity and bad theology like a coping mechanism, this book stands in open defiance. In *33 Days to Freedom From Lust*, Jared Moore shows what Scripture declares with blazing clarity: sound theology saves people, bad theology hurts people. Moore refuses to leave readers with the lie that lust is "inevitable" or "just part of being a man." Instead, he lifts our eyes to the God who is eternal, holy, all-powerful, all-knowing, and infinitely more satisfying than sin.

With pastoral precision, Moore works out the truth that the only power strong enough to expel lust is the expulsive power of a greater affection, joy in Christ Himself. This book does not tell men to "try harder." It calls them to enjoy Christ more. Page after page redirects the heart to the beauty, glory, and sufficiency of God.

There is hope. The temptation to sexual immorality can be killed by looking to Christ. Not by white-knuckled effort, but by beholding the Savior who conquered sin, breaks chains, and satisfies the deepest longings of the soul. You were made for worship and only Christ delivers freedom.

This is more than a devotional. It is war manual guided by theology that actually works.

— **Dusty Deevers**

Oklahoma State Senator
Pastor, Grace Community Church, Elgin, OK

When we read about the "7 Deadly Sins" we tend to rank them in terms of perceived manageability. 'Sloth'—manageable; 'Pride'—challenging, but still manageable; but 'Lust'?—give up, it's hopeless, especially in today's super-sensual world.

Jared Moore with *33 Days to Freedom from Lust* says, not so fast. There's hope. But freedom from lust won't come fast. It will take time, and discipline, and attention, and most of all, the grace of God. I encourage you to pick up this book and apply yourself to what it prescribes. Scripture and prayer have been known to work wonders.

— **C. R. Wiley**

Senior Editor, *Touchstone* Magazine
Co-host, *The Theology Pugcast*

A joyful journey from sin to obedience for men and women seeking to mortify the sin of lust. Indeed, most of the principles Dr. Moore teaches are helpful for mortifying any sin. I appreciate the thoughtful and organized way the book is structured, and its multi-sensory approach designed to help the reader internalize each precept. This book is a must have for biblical counseling and discipleship.

— **Michelle Lesley**

Women's discipleship blogger/speaker
Co-host, *A Word Fitly Spoken Podcast*

Jared tackles one of, if not the most tempting and destructive sins in men's lives, lust. This book will ground you on the rock of Jesus Christ, through Biblical truth. If you want to find freedom from sexual temptation, porn, lustful thoughts and actions, this is a resource that will lead you down the path of righteousness and equip you with the tools to not only fight the battle against lust, but defeat it by the grace of God Almighty.

— **Jon Root**

Faith, Sports and Culture Commentator
Content Creator, Host, Writer

The best way to kill sin is to hate it. And the best way to hate sin is to love and fear God. That's what *33 Days to Freedom From Lust* is all about. Dr. Moore's book is not about coddling people in their sin nor hammering them with guilt. Rather, Moore's book is a scripture saturated guide into the character and beauty of God with an eye to cultivate the kind of deep affection for God that can overwhelm and ultimately mortify the sin of lust. Moore's approach is refreshingly holistic. Each brief chapter will help readers cultivate a deeper affection for God through prayer, scripture readings, poetry, music, and practical application, the cumulative effects of which will equip the dedicated saint to fight, and ultimately overcome, the sin of lust. Highly recommend.

— **Michael Clary**

Author, *God's Good Design*
Pastor, Christ the King Church, Fort Thomas, KY

In *33 Days to Freedom from Lust*, Dr. Jared Moore takes a very different, but thoroughly biblical approach to the struggle of lust that has plagued so many men. Dr. Moore asserts that this struggle against immorality is not an ever-present battle by which all men must continue to suffer without end, but rather, is a battle that can be conquered through the power of God made available to all who call upon the name of the Lord. This thirty-three-day devotional is not only saturated with great Scripture references, worthy of memorization and meditation, Dr. Moore also includes a different hymn and even a poem each day that reflects on God's greatness from that day's passage. Throughout this book, the reader will find biblically faithful commentary to accompany the verses he cites, along with incisive applications that will challenge, convict, and transform all who are willing to follow this devotional plan faithfully. What I perhaps loved most of all was the focus upon the great attributes of the triune God, which should never get old for those desiring to grow in their knowledge of the Holy One. Dr. Moore shows that the value of knowing such attributes stretches far beyond just mental assent but extends practically and powerfully to the daily battles of Christian life. This is a resource I plan on using in my own pastoral ministries.

— **Ekkie Tepsupornchai**

Pastor, Western Avenue Baptist Church, Brawley, CA

Lust is a pernicious sin that is ravaging the church today. It wrecks marriages, dulls the soul, hardens the heart, and degrades men and women made in the image of God. In *33 Days to Freedom From Lust*, Moore takes aim at this relentless enemy by providing a hope-filled battle plan. This daily devotional is accessible yet substantive, practical yet concise. I plan to use it in my pastoral counseling, and I commend it as a valuable tool for those who seek to put to death the deeds of the flesh.

— **Dr. Jon English Lee**

Academic Dean and Professor of Systematic and Historical Theology, Covenant Baptist Theological Seminary, Owensboro, KY

Lust is one of the most pervasive threats to Christian holiness in our age. As a pastor, I regularly counsel men and women who wrestle with this sin, often for many years. What many need is a practical, hope-filled path forward. Dr. Jared Moore's *33 Days to Freedom from Lust* provides exactly that—an accessible, useful, and deeply biblical guide that helps readers build both spiritual and practical strategies to fight temptation and pursue purity for the glory of God. I gladly commend this devotional to pastors for counseling, to parents for discipleship with their children, and to every believer who desires to strengthen their resolve to live a holy and pure life before the Lord.

— **Dr. Ethan Jago**

Lead Pastor, 5 Bridges Church, Panama City Beach, FL

In a culture that excuses lust as natural and inevitable, many Christians have accepted a powerless view of sanctification. Even in the church, lust is often treated as an uncontrollable urge rather than a sin to be mortified through the Spirit. The result is hopelessness and bondage as believers try to manage sin instead of putting it to death.

Dr. Jared Moore's *33 Days to Freedom from Lust* exposes that lie and points us back to the God who truly satisfies. By comparing the false promises of lust with the character of God Himself, Moore lifts our gaze from the pit of self-gratification to the glory of the Triune God. He offers not just theological reflection but a pattern of repentance, worship, and renewal through Scripture, prayer, application, poems, and songs. This book is a full-orbed call to reorient the mind, heart, and life around the truth of God's Word.

As a biblical counselor, I found this devotional both rigorous and deeply pastoral. Moore doesn't merely tell readers to "stop sinning," he shows how the knowledge of God displaces the false worship that fuels lust. He treats lust not as a habit to manage but as an idol to destroy through greater affection for Christ. I especially appreciate how this book demonstrates that spiritual disciplines fuel obedience, but they don't replace it. That truth resounds implicitly through every page. The structure of daily meditation, reflection, and response makes this resource not only instructive but formational as it trains the reader's affections toward holiness.

If you're weary of confessing the same sin without real change, or if you counsel others who feel trapped in lust, this book belongs in your hands. Don't settle for coping with sin when Christ offers freedom. *33 Days to Freedom from Lust* is a guide for those ready to take sin seriously, love God supremely, and live in the freedom that only He can give.

— Nick Sevier

ACBC Certified Biblical Counselor
Founder and Director, Biblical Counselors Society

CONTENTS

Introduction

I grew up in an evangelical church that loved Jesus, His word, one another, and others. As teens, we were taught much good, truth, and beauty, but we were taught a few errors as well. One was the idea that, for men, lust is inevitable. It's just part of who you are in this fallen world, your sinful burden in this life. They did teach us not to act on the lust, but it would be there our whole lives.

My church was right that you don't have to act on your indwelling lusts, but they were wrong in telling us that inward lusting was part of being a man. Adam didn't lust before the Fall (Gen 2). Jesus didn't lust (2 Cor 5:21). And you don't have to lust. No Christian man or woman has to lust.

In the power of the Holy Spirit, you can put lust to death in your heart. Remember what Paul wrote to the Christians at Rome and Colosse, "If by the Spirit you put to death the deeds of the body, you will live" (Rom 8:13); and, "Put to death therefore what is earthly in you: sexual immorality, impurity, passion, evil desire, and covetousness, which is idolatry" (Col 3:5).

That's why I wrote this devotional: to give you hope.

My prayer is that as you read God's Word, the Bible, and you receive it, believe it, and live it, your thoughts will be more and more obedient to Christ. You will think God's thoughts after Him, which will bring you victory over your indwelling lusts and other sins in your heart.

Now, in this life, there must be sin in Christians, because our flesh is full of sin (Rom 7), but our flesh does not have to desire the same particular sins continually. By the power of the Holy Spirit, we can put to death particular lusts of our flesh. But how?

We must develop holy habits by thinking God's thoughts after Him and having greater affection for God than we do for lust. By the Holy Spirit's power, we create new habits by starving the lust in our hearts when it moves, one day at a time, until it's starved to death and a new holy habit is formed. According to some scientific studies, the least time to form a new habit is 21 days, with the average being 66 days. Thus, I chose 33 days to freedom from lust because it's greater than 21 days and half of 66 days.[1]

For some of you, 33 days will be enough for you to repent and form new holy habits. For others, you may need to repeat this book twice, or your second read can focus on memorizing the Freedom From Lust Shorter and Larger Catechisms. The goal is to develop greater affection for God, Christ, the Holy Spirit, and His morals, and to increase in your hatred for your lust and sin.

Are you ready to leave lust behind?

---

[1] Phillippa Lally, Cornelia H. M. Van Jaarsveld, Henry W. W. Potts, and Jane Wardle, "How are habits formed: Modeling habit formation in the real world," *European Journal of Social Psychology* 40, no. 6 (2010): 998-1009, https://onlinelibrary.wiley.com/doi/abs/10.1002/ejsp.674.

How to Use This Book

This 33-day devotional is written for Christians, to help you repent of lust at the root before it takes over your life and severely harms you and others. If you're not a Christian, you must turn from your sin and trust in Jesus Christ as Savior and Lord and commit the rest of your life to live for Him. You must believe that He died for your sins and rose from the dead to forgive you your sins. Through faith in Christ, God declares you righteous, crediting you with His Son's righteousness.

Only when you believe in Jesus will you receive the Holy Spirit and be strengthened to put your sin to death at the root. When we become Christians, God frees our wills from having to submit to our flesh. He enables us to walk with the Holy Spirit, living out the fruit He is producing in us. Without salvation in Christ and the sanctifying work of the Holy Spirit, you can only trade one sin for another, lust for self-righteousness or for something else.

Each day of this devotion follows the same sanctifying structure:
- Begin with Prayer
- Scripture and Reflection
- Application
- Marching Orders, Thinking God's Thoughts After Him:
    o One Sentence to Shape Your Affections
    o One Poem to Shape Your Affections
    o One Song to Shape Your Affections
- End with Prayer

Begin with Prayer: Through prayer, we show our faith, and we depend on God for our salvation, sanctification, and everything else we need.

Scripture and Reflection: As we read, believe, and receive Scripture, the Holy Spirit conforms us to the image of Christ.

Application: We must take responsibility to apply to our lives what God's word says from our hearts.

Marching Orders: Like a soldier headed into battle, we must submit to the orders of our Superior. God is our sovereign Ruler. We must heed His word to train and shape our affections by taking responsibility to think God's thoughts after Him, as we make war against our flesh and the evil one.

One sentence to shape your affections: We can train our affections through memorizing and thinking on one summary sentence of God's truth.

One poem to shape your affections: We can train our affections by memorizing truth that comes from God's word. Memorizing poems is often easier than memorizing paragraphs.

One song to shape your affections: We can train our affections by meditating on Scripture and the truth built upon it, by hearing and singing God's word often.[2]

End with Prayer: Through prayer, we trust and depend upon God to give us victory over lust and other motions of sin, and to think His thoughts after Him.

Let's get started enjoying God, Christ, and the Holy Spirit, and fighting and killing indwelling lust.

---

[2] If you would like a playlist of the 33 songs referenced in this devotional, you can find it at Jared's YouTube channel, "Dr. Jared Moore." The playlist is titled, "33 Days to Freedom From Lust." Or you can follow this direct link, https://www.youtube.com/watch?v=YXE7YDchhDM&list=PLOk-LGYpzz-qOBTJLvqjI_EasDlRAva-t.

Day 1

God is Eternal / Lust is Temporary

Begin with Prayer

Scripture and Reflection

Genesis 1:1 – In the beginning, God created the heavens and the earth (ESV).

Psalm 90:2 – Before the mountains were brought forth, or ever you had formed the earth and the world, from everlasting to everlasting you are God.

Isaiah 44:6 – Thus says the Lord, the King of Israel and his Redeemer, the Lord of hosts: "I am the first and I am the last; besides me there is no god."

Revelation 1:8 – "I am the Alpha and the Omega," says the Lord God, "who is and who was and who is to come, the Almighty."

God has no beginning, but everything else does. God has always been and always will be. As Moses prayed, "from everlasting to everlasting you are God" (Ps 90:2). God has no end.

Deuteronomy 6:4 – "Hear, O Israel: The Lord our God, the Lord is one."

1 John 4:8 – Anyone who does not love does not know God, because God is love.

19

God is only one Nature. He has no parts. Therefore, He is not the sum of His parts. All that God is, He is 100%. He is 100% God always and forever, never changing.

Exodus 3:14 – God said to Moses, "I am who I am." And he said, "Say this to the people of Israel: 'I am has sent me to you.'"

Psalm 102:25-27 – 25 Of old you laid the foundation of the earth, and the heavens are the work of your hands. 26 They will perish, but you will remain; they will all wear out like a garment. You will change them like a robe, and they will pass away, 27 but you are the same, and your years have no end.

God exists in and of Himself from eternity past. He is self-existing and has no needs. All creation has a beginning and will have an end, but God is everlasting.

Application

When you lust, you sin against the only One in all creation who has no needs. The God who had no need for creating, freely chose to create all things, except sin, which the devil and man created by misusing God's creation (Gen 3:1-6).

God calls us to worship Him with our entire lives. We need Him. He does not need us. Our lives and our breath, and our worship of Him, are privileges. The privilege is all ours.

Receiving and knowing God through Christ, and knowing these privileges that He has given us, how can we give ourselves to that which is contrary to Him? How can we give ourselves to what the devil and Adam created (Rom 5:12), to what is temporary and fleeting, the lust that is headed to hell, when God who has called us is eternal, unending, and calling us to Heaven?

He is worthy of our love and devotion. Lust is not.

Marching Orders: Thinking God's Thoughts After Him

Receive, Believe, and live the truths you've read. Memorize and meditate on these truths today:

One Sentence to Shape Your Affections:

God is eternal, has no beginning, no end, no parts, no needs, and He exists in and of Himself from eternity past, now, and forever; while lust began in the serpent's heart, will end in the Lake of Fire, and only offers fleeting pleasure that quickly fades.

One Poem to Shape Your Affections:

God eternal, no start, no end,
No parts, no needs, we all on Him depend.
Past, now and forever, He simply is,
In Him, eternal bliss, my salvation begins.

But lust began in the serpent's heart,
And bids me, from God to depart.
Promising me bliss with a deathly kiss,
Its pleasures flee, as I hear the serpent hiss.

One Song to Shape Your Affections:

Add this song to your playlist, "Eternal God, Whose Power Upholds"

On YouTube,
By Melissa Oretade (Written by Henry Hallam Tweedy)

https://www.youtube.com/watch?v=YXE7YDehhDM

1. Eternal God, whose power upholds
Both flower and flaming star,

To whom there is no here nor there,
No time, no near nor far,
No alien race, no foreign shore,
No child unsought, unknown:
O send us forth, Thy prophets true,
To make all lands Thine own!

2. O God of love, whose Spirit wakes
In every human breast,
Whom love, and love alone, can know,
In whom all hearts find rest:
Help us to spread Thy gracious reign
Till greed and hate shall cease,
And kindness dwell in human hearts,
And all the earth find peace!

3. O God of truth, whom science seeks
And reverent souls adore,
Who lightest every earnest mind
Of every clime and shore:
Dispel the gloom of error's night,
Of ignorance and fear,
Until true wisdom from above
Shall make life's pathway clear!

4. O God of beauty, oft revealed
In dreams of human art,
In speech that flows to melody,
In holiness of heart:
Teach us to turn from sinfulness
That shuts our hearts to Thee,
Till all shall know the loveliness
Of lives made fair and free!

5. O God of righteousness and grace,
Seen in the Christ, Thy Son,
Whose life and death reveal Thy face,
By whom Thy will was done:
Inspire Thy heralds of good news
To live Thy life divine,
Till Christ has formed in all mankind
And every land is Thine![3]

End with Prayer

---

[3] "Eternal God, Whose Power Upholds," Hymnary, Accessed September 13, 2025, https://hymnary.org/text/eternal_god_whose_power_upholds.

Day 2

God is Holy / Lust is Sin

Begin with Prayer

Scripture and Reflection

<u>Psalm 139:1-6</u> –

O LORD, you have searched me and known me! [2] You know when I sit down and when I rise up; you discern my thoughts from afar. [3] You search out my path and my lying down and are acquainted with all my ways. [4] Even before a word is on my tongue, behold, O LORD, you know it altogether. [5] You hem me in, behind and before, and lay your hand upon me. [6] Such knowledge is too wonderful for me; it is high; I cannot attain it.

<u>Psalm 145:3</u> – Great is the LORD, and greatly to be praised, and his greatness is unsearchable.

<u>Isaiah 55:8-9</u> – [8] For my thoughts are not your thoughts, neither are your ways my ways, declares the LORD. [9] For as the heavens are higher than the earth, so are my ways higher than your ways and my thoughts than your thoughts.

God is incomprehensible, which means that He is beyond our full understanding. He is Holy. He is other than His creation because He is the Creator. He knows Himself perfectly, but we only know Him based on what He's decided to tell us and how He's made us capable of understanding Him.

He has revealed Himself to us clearly in the Bible through the prophets, apostles (and their close associates), and Jesus Christ (Ps 119; 2 Tim 3:16-17). God transcends us in all His knowledge: of Himself and creation. He knows more and better than we do about all things because His knowledge is wider and deeper than our knowledge.

Isaiah 6:1-7 –

> In the year that King Uzziah died I saw the Lord sitting upon a throne, high and lifted up; and the train of his robe filled the temple. ² Above him stood the seraphim. Each had six wings: with two he covered his face, and with two he covered his feet, and with two he flew. ³ And one called to another and said: "Holy, holy, holy is the LORD of hosts; the whole earth is full of his glory!" ⁴ And the foundations of the thresholds shook at the voice of him who called, and the house was filled with smoke. ⁵ And I said: "Woe is me! For I am lost; for I am a man of unclean lips, and I dwell in the midst of a people of unclean lips; for my eyes have seen the King, the LORD of hosts!" ⁶ Then one of the seraphim flew to me, having in his hand a burning coal that he had taken with tongs from the altar. ⁷ And he touched my mouth and said: "Behold, this has touched your lips; your guilt is taken away, and your sin atoned for."

God is morally pure. He is holy of Himself, morally set apart from His creation. He is all good, perfectly righteous. Isaiah, the holy and righteous prophet, who was living among a wicked people, understood that he was truly *unholy* and *unrighteous* when he came into God's presence. If God did not cleanse him of his sin, he would not be clean.

God's holiness exposed Isaiah's unholiness or sin.

Application

When you lust, you're saying in your heart that you know both God and His creation better than He does. You're using yourself and others in ways that God didn't design, going against His revealed will in the Bible.

To lust, you must, in that moment, swap out God, who is perfectly good and holy, along with His wise design, for something that is unholy and unrighteous, and foolish. It's like a child on Christmas morning who just opened awesome presents but immediately leaves to go outside and play in the garbage instead; such is the Christian who lusts.

Think about it: why would you choose lust? Why embrace or justify something you can understand, knowing it won't satisfy you, something you weren't created for, over the One who's greater than our understanding? He can satisfy you with His perfect goodness and wants only good for you (Rom 8:28). How could you choose evil and foolishness, even if just for a moment?

Marching Orders: Thinking God's Thoughts After Him

Receive, believe, and live the truths you've read. Memorize and meditate on these truths today:

One Sentence to Shape Your Affections:

God is beyond my full understanding and knows more and better than I do, yet He has revealed Himself to me through creation and the Bible, showing me His perfect goodness, which exposes lust as empty and unable to satisfy me.

One Poem to Shape Your Affections:

God, beyond my grasp, yet finitely known,
The Creator, not of flesh and bone.
Yet through prophets, apostles, and Christ's grace,
In creation and Scripture, He reveals His face.

His wisdom vast, His insight pure,
He knows better and more than me, I am sure.
His righteousness revealed, all good is He,
In perfect holiness, His essence be.

But lust, my life, it soils,
And my relationship with God, it spoils.
Emptiness is its nature, and all it does bring,
Twists my senses deaf, I can't hear creation sing.

One Song to Shape Your Affections:

Add this song to your playlist, "My Soul, Thy Great Creator Praise" (Selections from Psalm 104)

On YouTube,
By Brian Sauvé (Written by Isaac Watts)
(8 verses. The full song is 28 verses)

https://www.youtube.com/watch?v=cgyRPrMLVX8

1. My soul, thy great Creator praise;
When cloth'd in his celestial rays,
He in full majesty appears,
And like a robe his glory wears.

2. The heav'ns are for his curtains spread;
The unfathomed deep he makes his bed.
Clouds are his chariot when he flies
On winged storms across the skies.

3. Angels, whom his own breath inspires,
His ministers, are flaming fires;

And swift as thought their armies move
To bear his vengeance or his love.

4. Vast are thy works, almighty Lord,
All nature rests upon thy word,
And the whole race of creatures stands,
Waiting their portion from thy hands.

5. But when thy face is hid they mourn,
And dying to their dust return;
Both man and beast their souls resign;
Life, breath and spirit, all are thine.

6. Yet thou canst breathe on dust again,
And fill the world with beasts and men;
A word of thy creating breath
Repairs the wastes of time and death.

7. In thee my hopes and wishes meet,
And make my meditations sweet:
Thy praises shall my breath employ
Till it expire in endless joy.

8. While haughty sinners die accurst,
Their glory buri'd with their dust,
I to my God my heav'nly King,
Immortal hallelujahs sing.[4]

End with Prayer

---

[4] "The Glory of God in Creation and Providence," Hymnary, Accessed September 13, 2025, https://hymnary.org/text/my_soul_thy_great_creator_praise.

Day 3

God is All Powerful / Lust is Weak

Begin with Prayer

Scripture and Reflection

<u>Genesis 1:1</u> – In the beginning, God created the Heavens and the Earth.

<u>Genesis 17:1</u> – When Abram was ninety-nine years old the Lord appeared to Abram and said to him, "I am God Almighty; walk before me, and be blameless,"

<u>Job 42:1-2</u> – Then Job answered the Lord and said: [2] "I know that you can do all things, and that no purpose of yours can be thwarted."

God is Creator, making all things out of nothing. Everything else, except sin, is His creation. He is all powerful. Look around you at His creation and see the clear evidence of His unlimited power.

The largest star in our galaxy, the Milky Way, is called UY Scuti. It's 5,000,000,000 times larger than the sun and 7,000,000,000,000,000 times larger than the earth.[5] Why did God create UY Scuti? To show us what small is, and to give us a glimpse of what all-powerful means. God is infinitely greater than UY Scuti and all the rest of creation.

---

[5] Colin Stuart, "Star UY Scuti is so big, you could fit 5 billion Suns inside it," Sky at Night Magazine, February 26, 2024, https://www.skyatnightmagazine.com/space-science/uy-scuti.

[After God permitted Satan to take Job's children, servants, and his possessions]
Job 1:20-21 – [20] Then Job arose and tore his robe and shaved his head and fell on the ground and worshiped. [21] And he said, "Naked I came from my mother's womb, and naked shall I return. The Lord gave, and the Lord has taken away; blessed be the name of the Lord."

Psalm 115:2-3 – [2] Why should the nations say, "Where is their God?" [3] Our God is in the heavens; he does all that he pleases.

Isaiah 55:10-11 –
> [10] "For as the rain and the snow come down from heaven and do not return there but water the earth, making it bring forth and sprout, giving seed to the sower and bread to the eater, [11] so shall my word be that goes out from my mouth; it shall not return to me empty, but it shall accomplish that which I purpose, and shall succeed in the thing for which I sent it.

Jeremiah 32:17 – 'Ah, Lord God! It is you who have made the heavens and the earth by your great power and by your outstretched arm! Nothing is too hard for you.

Revelation 19:6-8 –
> [6] Then I heard what seemed to be the voice of a great multitude, like the roar of many waters and like the sound of mighty peals of thunder, crying out, "Hallelujah! For the Lord our God the Almighty reigns. [7] Let us rejoice and exult and give him the glory, for the marriage of the Lamb has come, and his Bride has made herself ready; [8] it was granted her to clothe herself with fine linen, bright and pure"—for the fine linen is the righteous deeds of the saints.

God does all that He pleases. He gives and takes away and can do all His holy will. He has given His word directly, through the prophets, apostles (and their close associates), and Christ, for His own Divine purposes. And His word will not fail because He is all powerful and cannot fail.

Application

When you lust, you sin against your Creator. He made you and everything else for His glory. To lust you must use what God created in a way that is contrary to Him. Therefore, lust is an attempt to play God, to pretend like you determine the design and purpose for yourself and others.

Not only that, but when you lust, you sin against the One who is all powerful. You go against His design and purpose for you and others. He gives you life and holds your life in His hands, and the rest of creation.

Do you have a healthy fear of your Creator? Or do you have no fear of the One who is all powerful? He can prosper you or take you out of this life at any time. And He determines the reward and loss of reward for all Christians in the New Heavens and New Earth (1 Cor 3:12-15).

Marching Orders: Thinking God's Thoughts After Him

Receive, believe, and live the truths you've read. Memorize and meditate on these truths today:

One Sentence to Shape Your Affections:

God is Creator, doing whatever He pleases, accomplishing His holy will by giving His word, and giving and taking life for His own glory; while lust has no power over me unless I permit it.

One Poem to Shape Your Affections:

God, the almighty Creator,
Designer of all that's good.
Of sin alone, He is not the Maker,
His power is everywhere understood.

He acts with sovereign purpose, high and free,
Gives and takes by His decree.

His timeless word, true and bright,
Given in the Bible, His truth is light.

But lust needs my permission,
A cancer to grow without remission.
This parasite eats my heart into a crater,
Drinking my life away, as it mocks my Creator.

One Song to Shape Your Affections:

Add this song to your playlist, "Whate'er My God Ordains is Right"

On YouTube,
By Sovereign Grace Music (Written by Samuel Rodigast)

https://www.youtube.com/watch?v=z-yJ3xMVUDI

1. Whate'er my God ordains is right,
Holy His will abideth.
I will be still whate'er He does,
And follow where He guideth.
He is my God,
Though dark my road.
He holds me that I shall not fall
Wherefore to Him I leave it all

2. Whate'er my God ordains is right,
He never will deceive me
He leads me by the proper path,
I know He will not leave me
I take, content,
What He hath sent
His hand can turn my griefs away
And patiently I wait His day

3. Whate'er my God ordains is right,
Though now this cup in drinking
May bitter seem to my faint heart,
I take it all unshrinking
My God is true,
Each morn anew
Sweet comfort yet shall fill my heart
And pain and sorrow shall depart.

4. Whate'er my God ordains is right,
Here shall my stand be taken
Though sorrow, need, or death be mine,
Yet I am not forsaken
My Father's care
Is round me there
He holds me that I shall not fall
And so to Him I leave it all.[6]

End with Prayer

---

[6] "Whate'er My God Ordains is Right," Hymnary, Accessed September 13, 2025, https://hymnary.org/text/whateer_my_god_ordains_is_right_holy_his.

Day 4

God is All Knowing / Lust Knows Only Death

Begin with Prayer

Scripture and Reflection

Isaiah 41:21-24 –

> 21 Set forth your case, says the LORD; bring your proofs, says the King of Jacob. 22 Let them bring them, and tell us what is to happen. Tell us the former things, what they are, that we may consider them, that we may know their outcome; or declare to us the things to come. 23 Tell us what is to come hereafter, that we may know that you are gods; do good, or do harm, that we may be dismayed and terrified. 24 Behold, you are nothing, and your work is less than nothing; an abomination is he who chooses you.

At this time, Israel and Judah were two separate nations, but both were worshipping false gods. God permitted Israel to fall, and the Assyrians marched towards Judah, seeking to destroy it. But God spared Judah, showing His omniscience in a way no false god could.

Only the true God can change history, because He alone knows the beginning, end, and all that comes in-between. Herein lies the proof of His divinity: He is all knowing and exposes the deception of all other gods. They are ignorant of the future and are powerless to change it.

Matthew 11:20-24 –

[20] Then he [Jesus] began to denounce the cities where most of his mighty works had been done, because they did not repent. [21] "Woe to you, Chorazin! Woe to you, Bethsaida! For if the mighty works done in you had been done in Tyre and Sidon, they would have repented long ago in sackcloth and ashes. [22] But I tell you, it will be more bearable on the day of judgment for Tyre and Sidon than for you. [23] And you, Capernaum, will you be exalted to heaven? You will be brought down to Hades. For if the mighty works done in you had been done in Sodom, it would have remained until this day. [24] But I tell you that it will be more tolerable on the day of judgment for the land of Sodom than for you."

1 Corinthians 2:7-8 – [7] But we impart a secret and hidden wisdom of God, which God decreed before the ages for our glory. [8] None of the rulers of this age understood this, for if they had, they would not have crucified the Lord of glory.

God knows all that is knowable or all that can be known, past, present, and future. He knows all that will be and all possibilities that could be throughout all time and space. He cannot learn. Learning is something only a creature can do, not the Creator. His knowledge is not acquired; it's inherent. He knows all things from eternity past.

Ecclesiastes 6:12 – For who knows what is good for man while he lives the few days of his vain life, which he passes like a shadow? For who can tell man what will be after him under the sun?

God, who has always been and always will be and who is all-knowing, knows what is best for mankind. But what does a man know? We are only here for a little while. We pass like a shadow. And if God doesn't speak, who can tell us about the future? No one.

If we look at the history of mankind, it brings hollow hopes. Our past cannot save us, nor can the knowledge we've learned. History seems to keep repeating itself. There is much evil in the past of mankind. And it does not bring hope about the future.

But God, the One who knows all things, He is our hope. He transcends our finite history and offers us a future that isn't shaped by our past but is rather transformed by His perfect design.

Psalm 46:1-3 – God is our refuge and strength, a very present help in trouble. ² Therefore we will not fear though the earth gives way, though the mountains be moved into the heart of the sea, ³ though its waters roar and foam, though the mountains tremble at its swelling. *Selah*

Christians sometimes think, "If I knew why God did this or permitted it, I would be happy or joyful." Yet, the Psalmist tells us that God is our refuge, strength, and our very present help in time of trouble. God is with us. And He knows all things. He knows why, which means we know the One who knows why, by the Spirit, through the Son, to the Father. Knowing Him is enough.

He brings comfort, knowing "why" does not. And obedience to Him brings joy and flourishing.

Application

God, the One who is all knowing, gave us a book that tells us how to flourish in His creation. His word is sufficient for all that we face in this life, including lust, precisely because He knows all things. The Bible gives us the moral answers for all things for all time.

When you lust, you must say in your heart that your knowledge is greater or better than God's knowledge. You must assume that you know more than God. Otherwise, you would do what He says, regardless of what your flesh or the world says.

When you lust, you put your trust in the mirror over the Master. Pursuing lust can only end poorly for you because, as God's word tells us, sin always leads to the grave (Rom 6:23; James 1:14-15). Sin cannot lead to life, joy, or happiness; it can only end in death.

To lust is to take a step toward the grave, or even to step into it; but to turn from lust is to turn to eternal life in God, by the Spirit, through the Son, to the Father.

Marching Orders: Thinking God's Thoughts After Him

Receive, believe, and live the truths you've read. Memorize and meditate on these truths today:

One Sentence to Shape Your Affections:

Only God knows all that has been, will be, could have been or could be, and He gave me some of His knowledge in the Bible, exactly what I need so that I will flourish; therefore, lust is and can only be the path to failure.

One Poem to Shape Your Affections:

God knows all that can be known,
Past and future, He alone.
Learning's not for Him, the Creator,
Master of all knowledge, none greater.

What does man know? A fleeting breath,
Here for a moment, and then death.
Without God's voice to light my way,
Lust and death await me each day.

But God, my beacon, hope, and guide,
In His knowledge I safely abide.
He knows what's best for mankind,

In Him, truth and love, I always find.

One Song to Shape Your Affections:

Add this song to your playlist, "His Mercy Is More"

On YouTube,
Song by Sovereign Grace Music (Written by Matt Papa and Matt Boswell)

https://www.youtube.com/watch?v=uh1KDpg00x8

[Due to copyright laws, I cannot include the lyrics here, but they are included in the above video.]

End with Prayer

Day 5

God is All Present / Lust is Only in Sinners

Begin with Prayer

Scripture and Reflection

Genesis 1:1 – In the beginning, God created the heavens and the earth.

God has always lived, even before creation. He is the Creator and is independent from His creation. Creation needs Him. He does not need His creation. "Need" is a word that describes creatures, not God.

Psalm 139:7-10 – 7 Where shall I go from your Spirit? Or where shall I flee from your presence? 8 If I ascend to heaven, you are there! If I make my bed in Sheol, you are there! 9 If I take the wings of the morning and dwell in the uttermost parts of the sea, 10 even there your hand shall lead me, and your right hand shall hold me.

Proverbs 15:3 – The eyes of the Lord are in every place, keeping watch on the evil and the good.

Jeremiah 23:23-24 – 23 "Am I a God at hand, declares the Lord, and not a God far away? 24 Can a man hide himself in secret places so that I cannot see him? Declares the Lord. Do I not fill heaven and earth? Declares the Lord."

Acts 17:24-28 –

> [24] The God who made the world and everything in it, being Lord of heaven and earth, does not live in temples made by man, [25] nor is he served by human hands, as though he needed anything, since he himself gives to all mankind life and breath and everything. [26] And he made from one man every nation of mankind to live on all the face of the earth, having determined allotted periods and the boundaries of their dwelling place, [27] that they should seek God, and perhaps feel their way toward him and find him. Yet he is actually not far from each one of us, [28] for "'In him we live and move and have our being'; as even some of your own poets have said, "'For we are indeed his offspring.'

Romans 8:38-39 – [38] For I am sure that neither death nor life, nor angels nor rulers, nor things present nor things to come, nor powers, [39] nor height nor depth, nor anything else in all creation, will be able to separate us from the love of God in Christ Jesus our Lord.

God, being greater than His creation, He is outside of time and space. Yet, He has chosen to freely fill all of time and space. No one can hide from God. He sees all things, whether good or evil.

And nothing can separate a Christian from God, nothing in heaven, nothing on earth. God could separate from us, but He won't. Why? Because He has freely poured out His love on His people through Christ Jesus our Lord, and He has told us that He will never separate from us (Rom 8:38-39; Phil 1:6).

Application

When you lust, you sin in God's presence. Though you cannot see Him, He always sees you.

When you lust in secret, you show that you are more concerned about what mankind thinks than what God sees and knows about you. You're more concerned with others *thinking* you're godly than *truly* being godly, because God sees you and you love and want to please Him.

It's a dangerous place for a Christian to be, who cares more about what people think than what God thinks (2 Sam 11-12). If this describes you, then you have a man-pleasing idol in your heart. As long as no one finds out, you'll be open to commit any sin.

Repent of your hypocrisy and your lust and get up and live for Jesus from your heart. He is worthy of our repentance. Strive to please Him above everyone else, and you'll leave your hypocrisy and lust behind, killing them at the root.

Marching Orders: Thinking God's Thoughts After Him

Receive, believe, and live the truths you've read. Memorize and meditate on these truths today:

One Sentence to Shape Your Affections:

God is independent from His creation, though He freely fills all time and space, and no one can hide from His presence or be ripped from His love in Christ; while lust is only present in sinners and will not exist in eternity with Jesus.

One Poem to Shape Your Affections:

God does not need what He has made,
For creation only exists in His shade.
He forever reigns outside His design,
Yet fills each moment, all of time.

No man can hide from God's infinite being,
His presence, His love, He is all-seeing.
He loves His church in Christ without end,
A bond that finite lust can never rend.

One Song to Shape Your Affections:

Add this song to your playlist, "The All-Seeing God."

On YouTube

By the Stutzman Family Singers (Written by Isaac Watts)

https://www.youtube.com/watch?v=VSYVgnwNgJ0

1. Lord, Thou hast searched and seen me through;
Thine eye commands, with piercing view,
My rising and my resting hours,
My heart and flesh, with all their powers.

2. Within Thy circling power I stand,
On every side I find Thy hand:
Awake, asleep, at home, abroad,
I am surrounded still with God.

3. Could I so false, so faithless prove,
To quit Thy service and Thy love,
Where Lord, could I Thy presence shun,
Or from Thy dreadful glory run?

4. The veil of night is no disguise,
No screen from Thy all-searching eyes;
Thy hand can seize Thy foes as soon
Through midnight shades, as blazing noon.

5. O may these thoughts possess my breast,
Where'er I rove, where'er I rest!
Nor let my weaker passions dare
Consent to sin, for God is there.[7]

End with Prayer

---

[7] "The All-Seeing God," Hymnary, Accessed September 13, 2025, https://hymnary.org/text/lord_thou_hast_searched_and_seen_me_thro.

Day 6

God is All Wise / Lust is All Stupid

Begin with Prayer

Scripture and Reflection

Psalm 104:24 – O Lord, how manifold are your works! In wisdom have you made them all; the earth is full of your creatures.

Jeremiah 10:12 – It is he who made the earth by his power, who established the world by his wisdom, and by his understanding stretched out the heavens.

Romans 11:33-35 – 33 Oh, the depth of the riches and wisdom and knowledge of God! How unsearchable are his judgments and how inscrutable his ways! 34 "For who has known the mind of the Lord, or who has been his counselor" [Isaiah 40:13]? 35 "Or who has given a gift to him that he might be repaid" [Job 41:11]?

God has made all things in creation for His own glory. It all displays His wisdom. His ways are greater than our ways. We're so small and God so great that we cannot even begin to fully understand His decisions and ways. When we don't understand God's plans, the error is always with us, not with God.

No one has known God's mind or advised Him. He's God; we're not. He's wise, and the little wisdom that we have comes from Him alone. God knows why He created and what He is doing with creation, even when we don't understand.

We cannot offer God anything He does not already own, for everything in creation is His by right and design. We owe God, but He does not owe us anything. The only thing that we have brought to God that He did not give to us is our sin. Everything else in us, all that is good, true, and beautiful, came from Him.

In the Old Testament, Job questioned God after He permitted Satan to take his children, servants, wealth, and health. God responded in Job 38-41, which can be summarized by Job 38:36, "36 Who has put wisdom in the inward parts or given understanding to the mind?" And the answer to the question is, "God!"

Job 42:1-6 –

> Then Job answered the Lord and said: 2 "I know that you can do all things, and that no purpose of yours can be thwarted. 3 'Who is this that hides counsel without knowledge?' Therefore I have uttered what I did not understand, things too wonderful for me, which I did not know. 4 'Hear, and I will speak; I will question you, and you make it known to me.' 5 I had heard of you by the hearing of the ear, but now my eye sees you; 6 therefore I despise myself, and repent in dust and ashes."

After God's sharp rebuke of Job in Job 38-41, he recognized the error of his questioning. Our ability to reason and understand God, His creation, and our circumstances come from God. How then can we, the creatures, challenge the Creator when all virtues within us—goodness, truth, and beauty—come from Him? The only reason that we can even understand God, and formulate and ask questions, is because He has given us the ability. Where we lack the ability to understand His ways, the error is with us, because He is all wise.

Application

If you were God, would you do anything different? If the answer is "yes," then you think there is a better way to run God's creation. You think you're wiser than

God. But the Scriptures say that God knows *why* He has done and *what* He is doing. We should always trust Him.

When you lust, you seek to correct God's wisdom. To lust, you must say in your heart that God got it wrong when He forbade lust and reserved sexual desire and sexual activity for marriage (Gen 2; Matt 5:27-30). This, of course, is foolish. God is all wise, and lust is all stupid.

Marching Orders: Thinking God's Thoughts After Him

Receive, Believe, and live the truths you've read. Memorize and meditate on these truths today:

One Sentence to Shape Your Affections:

With no counsel, help, input from anyone, or learning, God wisely made and governs all things, while lust twists God's life-giving creation into sin and death.

One Poem to Shape Your Affections:

God's canvas vast, from glory done,
Each thread of creation, His wisdom spun.
Small I am, and vast is He,
Beyond His word, His wisdom, a mystery.

When I can't grasp at understanding,
It's my fault, not His planning.
No one can counsel His mind,
He is God, we are mankind.

No gift can I give to Him in return,
For all I know and am, from Him I learn.
My reason and quest to understand,
Are but gifts from His loving hand.

How dare I question my Creator's deeds,

When all that is good in me, from Him proceeds.

My reasoning, my thoughts, my very speech,

Are His gifts, yet if I lust, to Him I preach.

One Song to Shape Your Affections:

Add this song to your playlist, "Thy Will Be Done"

On YouTube,

By Indelible Grace Music (Written by Charlotte Elliott)

https://www.youtube.com/watch?v=T-NEWao2AI8

1. My God and Father! while I stray,

Far from my home in life's rough way,

Oh! teach me from my heart to say,

"Thy will be done!" "Thy will be done!"

2. If Thou shouldst call me to resign,

What most I prize, it ne'er was mine.

I only yield Thee what was Thine;

"Thy will be done!" "Thy will be done!"

3. If but my fainting heart be blest,

With Thy sweet Spirit for its guest,

My God! To Thee I leave the rest,

"Thy will be done!" "Thy will be done!"

4. Renew my will from day to day,

Blend it with Thine, and take away,

All now that makes it hard to say,

"Thy will be done!" "Thy will be done!"

5. Then when on earth I breathe no more,
The prayer oft mixed with tears before,
I'll sing upon a happier shore,
"Thy will be done!" "Thy will be done!"[8]

End with Prayer

---

[8] "Thy Will Be Done," Indelible Grace Hymn Book, Accessed September 13, 2025, http://hymnbook.igracemusic.com/hymns/thy-will-be-done.

Day 7

God is Just / Lust is Injustice

Begin with Prayer

Scripture and Reflection

Psalm 19:7-11 –

> [7] The law of the Lord is perfect, reviving the soul; the testimony of the Lord is sure, making wise the simple; [8] the precepts of the Lord are right, rejoicing the heart; the commandment of the Lord is pure, enlightening the eyes; [9] the fear of the Lord is clean, enduring forever; the rules of the Lord are true, and righteous altogether. [10] More to be desired are they than gold, even much fine gold; sweeter also than honey and drippings of the honeycomb. [11] Moreover, by them is your servant warned; in keeping them there is great reward.

Romans 7:12 – So the law is holy, and the commandment is holy and righteous and good.

1 Peter 1:14-16 – [14] As obedient children, do not be conformed to the passions of your former ignorance, [15] but as he who called you is holy, you also be holy in all your conduct, [16] since it is written, "You shall be holy, for I am holy" [Lev 19:2].

God is holy and just. He gave us His law, His word, to display His holy and just nature. Like Him, His word is good and brings unlimited good:

1) It revives our souls.
2) It makes wise the simple.
3) It rejoices our hearts.
4) It enlightens our eyes.
5) It endures forever.
6) It is righteousness altogether.
7) It is more valuable than gold.
8) It is sweeter than honey.
9) It warns us.
10) It brings great reward to those who keep it.

The eternal value of God's word is clear, and He rewards those who obey it. God gave His word so that everyone would reflect Him. He is just and He holds everyone accountable to His word. Since He is holy, He requires His people to be holy too. He loves His people, and He expects us to love Him as well. We demonstrate our love to Him by being obedient to His word from our hearts.

Application

When you lust, you mistakenly believe that lust can give you the good only God's word can: reviving, wisdom, rejoicing, enlightening, endurance, righteousness, value, sweetness, warning, and reward. However, lust actually brings the opposite: weakening, stupidity, weeping, darkness, death, injustice, vanity, bitterness, danger, and judgment. God is just and His word is just, but lust is injustice towards God and others.

When you lust, you also assume that God will not hold you accountable for it. After all, you wouldn't lust in front of God's visible presence, though He is with you always. Since lust is sin against God, from seed to deed, it can only bring death; it's always marching to death, your death and the death of others (James 1:13-17; 4:1-10).

Now, it's true that our sin, lust included, is imputed to Christ through faith in Him, meaning God holds Christ accountable for it, not us, concerning our salvation. God has forgiven our sin and given us Christ's righteousness through faith (Rom 4). Yet, God does hold us accountable for how we live as Christians, in this life and concerning our loss of reward when we get to Heaven (1 Cor 3:11-15, 4:5; 2 Cor 5:10). God cares how His people live.

Every time you lust, you trade some of your eternal reward for momentary satisfaction.

Marching Orders: Thinking God's Thoughts After Him

Receive, believe, and live the truths you've read. Memorize and meditate on these truths today:

One Sentence to Shape Your Affections:

God, being inherently holy and just, has crafted His word in the same vein; thus, He holds everyone accountable to live in obedience to it from our hearts; therefore, those who lust will suffer loss, and if possible, death and hell.

One Poem to Shape Your Affections:

Holy and just, my God stands supreme,
His law, His word, a glorious beam.
To display His nature, so pure so bright,
A perfect guide, both day and night.

Like Him, His word, a fountain of good,
Brings unlimited blessings, as only it could.
Just and holy, He calls me to be,
Mirroring His nature for all to see.
Fulfilled by Christ, the law and word,
Freeing me with His righteousness, like a bird.

He takes my lust, my heart of stone, away,
Gifts me His Spirit and a new heart, so I won't stray.

One Song to Shape Your Affections:

Add this song to your playlist, "Before the Throne of God Above."

On YouTube,
By Sovereign Grace Music (Written by Charitie Lees Smith)

https://www.youtube.com/watch?v=765E7b7dv9I

1. Before the throne of God above
I have a strong and perfect plea
A great High Priest whose name is love
Who ever lives and pleads for me
My name is graven on His hands
My name is written on His heart
I know that while in heav'n He stands
No tongue can bid me thence depart
No tongue can bid me thence depart

2. When Satan tempts me to despair
And tells me of the guilt within
Upward I look and see Him there
Who made an end to all my sin
Because the sinless Savior died
My sinful soul is counted free
For God the Just is satisfied
To look on Him and pardon me
To look on Him and pardon me

3. Behold Him there, the risen Lamb
My perfect, spotless Righteousness

The great unchangeable I AM
The King of glory and of grace
One with Himself, I cannot die
My soul is purchased by His blood
My life is hid with Christ on high
With Christ my Savior and my God
With Christ my Savior and my God[9]

End with Prayer

[9] "Before the Throne of God Above," Hymnary, Accessed September 13, 2025, https://hymnary.org/text/before_the_throne_of_god_above_i_have_a_#Author.

Day 8

God is True / Lust is a Liar

Begin with Prayer

Scripture and Reflection

Psalm 116:11 – I said in my alarm, "All mankind are liars."

The Psalmist says that all men are liars, a statement unique to this sin among many more in Scripture. Why are all men liars? Because, in order to be bent against God, one must be contrary to God, who is true. Every sinner, therefore, is inherently contrary to God. Thus, every man has deceit in his heart, and from it sprouts all manner of lust and sin.

Titus 1:2 – in hope of eternal life, which God, who never lies, promised before the ages began.

Hebrews 6:18 – so that by two unchangeable things, in which it is impossible for God to lie, we who have fled for refuge might have strong encouragement to hold fast to the hope set before us.

1 John 5:20 – And we know that the Son of God has come and has given us understanding, so that we may know him who is true; and we are in him who is true, in his Son Jesus Christ. He is the true God and eternal life.

All men are liars, but God never lies. He is true in His very nature, and it is utterly impossible for Him to lie. He is immutable, never changing.

Not only is God true and never changes in His being, He's also unchanging in His commitments. Every promise He makes, every covenant He enters, He fulfills without fail. He cannot do otherwise. God sent His Son, Jesus Christ, to give His church understanding "so that we may know Him who is true" (1 John 5:20). Through Jesus Christ, we come to know this truth, because God ordained Him for this purpose.

"And we are in Him who is true, in His Son Jesus Christ. He is the true God and eternal life" (1 John 5:20). There is only one true God, and we are in Him through our union with Jesus Christ, who is God the Son Incarnate.

John 8:44 – You are of your father the devil, and your will is to do your father's desires. He was a murderer from the beginning, and does not stand in the truth, because there is no truth in him. When he lies, he speaks out of his own character, for he is a liar and the father of lies.

The devil is a liar and has been a liar from the beginning. There is no truth in Him at all. In contrast, God is true. The devil is the father of lies, and mankind reflects his nature in their deceitful hearts.

But this should not be the case for Christians, for we have been saved from the devil and our flesh and have been given new hearts that love God by the Holy Spirit through the Son to the Father. In the power of the Holy Spirit, we can put to death every lust that springs forth from our lying hearts, and we can live holy lives.

Application

When you lust, you lie against God, against who He is. As His image-bearer, you were designed to mirror His holy character back to Him and to the angels, but your lust reflects the devil instead. Since God is true, only inclinations, thoughts, desires, and actions that are true, reflect Him.

When you lust, you also lie against what God has promised to those who love Him. You live and reflect that God sent Christ, not to unite you to Himself who is true, but rather to unite you to the evil one who is the father of lies.

Remember, lust is a liar, and the devil is a deceiver, but God is true, and all He does is true.

Marching Orders: Thinking God's Thoughts After Him

Receive, believe, and live the truths you've read. Memorize and meditate on these truths today:

One Sentence to Shape Your Affections:

God is true, and all that He does is true, and everything contrary to Him mirrors the devil, who is the father of lies; therefore, lust deceives, promising joy only to deliver suffering, sin, and death.

One Poem to Shape Your Affections:

God is true, unchanging, light,
While men are liars, lost in night.
Lust sprouts from my heart of sin,
It comes from within, where lies begin.

Yet God, His nature, is firm and sure,
His truth endures, steadfast, pure.
Promises made, He will not break,
His love, even life and death cannot shake.

God sent His Son, Jesus Christ,

To teach me truth, to give me sight.
Through Him, God's truth I see,
And now in Christ, I see me.

"In Him who is true," I boldly stand,
In Jesus Christ, the Son of Man.
He is the true God, being life without end,
Himself He gives, my heart and soul to mend.

One Song to Shape Your Affections:

Add this song to your playlist, "A Mighty Fortress."

On YouTube,
Song by Matt Boswell (Written by Martin Luther)

https://www.youtube.com/watch?v=oNeP7bGagqg

1. A mighty fortress is our God,
A bulwark never failing;
Our helper he amidst the flood
Of mortal ills prevailing.
For still our ancient foe
Doth seek to work us woe
His craft and power are great,
And armed with cruel hate
On earth is not his equal

2. Did we in our own strength confide
Our striving would be losing
Were not the right Man on our side
The man of God's own choosing
Dost ask who that may be?
Christ Jesus, it is he

The Lord of hosts, His name
From age to age the same
And He must win the battle

3. And though this world, with devils filled
Should threaten to undo us
We will not fear, for God hath willed
His truth to triumph through us
The Prince of Darkness grim
We tremble not for him
His rage we can endure
For lo, his doom is sure
One little word shall fell him

4. That word above all earthly powers,
No thanks to them, abideth
The Spirit and the gifts are ours
Through him who with us sideth
Let goods and kindred go
This mortal life also
The body they may kill
God's truth abideth still
His kingdom is forever[10]

End with Prayer

---

[10] "A Mighty Fortress," Hymnary, Accessed September 13, 2025,
https://hymnary.org/text/a_mighty_fortress_is_our_god_a_bulwark.

Day 9

God is Beauty / Lust is Ugly

Begin with Prayer

Scripture and Reflection

<u>Psalm 19:1</u> – The heavens declare the glory of God, and the sky above proclaims his handiwork.

<u>Psalm 27:4</u> – One thing have I asked of the Lord, that will I seek after: that I may dwell in the house of the Lord all the days of my life, to gaze upon the beauty of the Lord and to inquire in his temple.

<u>Psalm 50:1-2</u> – The Mighty One, God the Lord, speaks and summons the earth from the rising of the sun to its setting. [2] Out of Zion, the perfection of beauty, God shines forth.

<u>Ecclesiastes 3:11</u> – He has made everything beautiful in its time. Also, he has put eternity into man's heart, yet so that he cannot find out what God has done from the beginning to the end.

<u>Ezekiel 28:11-17</u> –

[11] Moreover, the word of the Lord came to me: [12] "Son of man, raise a lamentation over the king of Tyre, and say to him, Thus says the Lord God: "You were the signet of perfection, full of wisdom and perfect in beauty. [13] You were in Eden, the garden of God; every precious stone was your covering, sardius, topaz, and diamond, beryl, onyx, and jasper, sapphire,

emerald, and carbuncle; and crafted in gold were your settings and your engravings. On the day that you were created they were prepared. [14] You were an anointed guardian cherub. I placed you; you were on the holy mountain of God; in the midst of the stones of fire you walked. [15] You were blameless in your ways from the day you were created, till unrighteousness was found in you. [16] In the abundance of your trade you were filled with violence in your midst, and you sinned; so I cast you as a profane thing from the mountain of God, and I destroyed you, O guardian cherub, from the midst of the stones of fire. [17] Your heart was proud because of your beauty; you corrupted your wisdom for the sake of your splendor. I cast you to the ground; I exposed you before kings, to feast their eyes on you."

God is the designer of all things, the Creator whose beauty is reflected in His creation. Even the devil was created as beautiful and only became ugly when unrighteousness was found in him. God's creation is beautiful because He is beautiful. Out of Zion comes Jesus Christ, God's Son in the flesh, the perfection of beauty.

The very definition of beauty is God and all that He has designed. Many claim, "Beauty is in the eye of the beholder," which, if true, means if someone judges something or someone as beautiful, then it must be right. This makes beauty subjective and based on the opinions of men rather than the perfect word of God.

Solomon tells us in Ecclesiastes 3:11 that beauty is objective, meaning, it's fixed. God makes everything beautiful in its time, indicating that there is a Divine purpose for the times and seasons of life. Thus, we should understand that "Beauty is in the eye of God," not in the eye of the beholder.

We only know and see beauty when our hearts, minds, and judgments are in agreement with God and His word.

Application

When you lust, you silently say in your heart that God is not beautiful, and neither is His design. Lust turns beauty upside down. Instead of seeing God and His design as beautiful, your heart seeks to take His place, saying, "I'm beautiful, my desire is beautiful, and the object of my desire is beautiful," even though you're using yourself and others contrary to God and His design.

When you lust, you proclaim in your heart that immorality is beautiful, that lawlessness is alluring. To lust, you must align with darkness and oppose the Light. Your heart is saying the devil, and his ways are beautiful, and God and His ways are ugly.

To summarize, to lust is to be ugly, to desire ugliness, and to become uglier.

Marching Orders: Thinking God's Thoughts After Him

Receive, believe, and live the truths you've read. Memorize and meditate on these truths today:

One Sentence to Shape Your Affections:

God is beauty and His design is beautiful; thus, all that is contrary to Him and His design is inherently ugly; therefore, lust is ugly and is the pursuit of ugliness.

One Poem to Shape Your Affections:

From Zion, the Savior comes, Jesus Divine,
God's Son Incarnate, Beauty's true design.
Perfection embodied, in Him beauty's peak,
A testament to the Creator, heard by the humble and meek.

Yet voices around me, they whisper and say,
"Beauty's in the beholder," in a subjective way.
But this view is fleeting, like shadows at noon,

For beauty, true beauty, is not mine to assume.

Solomon in wisdom, in Ecclesiastes he penned,
That beauty is timeless, from God's hand to send.
Not by the eye of man, but by Divine sight,
Beauty is fixed, from God's perfect light.

So let me see beauty as God does define,
Not through my lustful vision, but His flawless design.
For all that He creates, in time, comes to be,
A reflection of His beauty, for all eternity.

One Song to Shape Your Affections:

Add this song to your playlist, "This is my Father's World."

On YouTube,
By Hymns of Grace (Written by Maltbie Babcock)

https://www.youtube.com/watch?v=-y93uhtTibM

1. This is my Father's world,
And to my listening ears
All nature sings, and round me rings
The music of the spheres.
This is my Father's world:
I rest me in the thought
Of rocks and trees, of skies and seas--
His hand the wonders wrought.

2. This is my Father's world:
The birds their carols raise,
The morning light, the lily white,
Declare their Maker's praise.

This is my Father's world:
He shines In all that's fair;
In the rustling grass I hear Him pass,
He speaks to me everywhere.

3. This is my Father's world:
O let me ne'er forget
That though the wrong seems oft so strong,
God is the Ruler yet.
This is my Father's world:
Why should my heart be sad?
The Lord is King: let the heavens ring!
God reigns; let earth be glad![11]

End with Prayer

[11] "This is my Father's World," Hymnary, Accessed September 13, 2025, https://hymnary.org/text/this_is_my_fathers_world_and_to_my.

Day 10

God is Love / Lust is Hate

Begin with Prayer

Scripture and Reflection

<u>Psalm 136:1-26</u> –

Give thanks to the Lord, for he is good,
    for his steadfast love endures forever.
[2] Give thanks to the God of gods,
    for his steadfast love endures forever.
[3] Give thanks to the Lord of lords,
    for his steadfast love endures forever;
[4] to him who alone does great wonders,
    for his steadfast love endures forever;
[5] to him who by understanding made the heavens,
    for his steadfast love endures forever;
[6] to him who spread out the earth above the waters,
    for his steadfast love endures forever;
[7] to him who made the great lights,
    for his steadfast love endures forever;
[8] the sun to rule over the day,
    for his steadfast love endures forever;
[9] the moon and stars to rule over the night,
    for his steadfast love endures forever;

¹⁰ to him who struck down the firstborn of Egypt,
      for his steadfast love endures forever;
¹¹ and brought Israel out from among them,
      for his steadfast love endures forever;
¹² with a strong hand and an outstretched arm,
      for his steadfast love endures forever;
¹³ to him who divided the Red Sea in two,
      for his steadfast love endures forever;
¹⁴ and made Israel pass through the midst of it,
      for his steadfast love endures forever;
¹⁵ but overthrew Pharaoh and his host in the Red Sea,
      for his steadfast love endures forever;
¹⁶ to him who led his people through the wilderness,
      for his steadfast love endures forever;
¹⁷ to him who struck down great kings,
      for his steadfast love endures forever;
¹⁸ and killed mighty kings,
      for his steadfast love endures forever;
¹⁹ Sihon, king of the Amorites,
      for his steadfast love endures forever;
²⁰ and Og, king of Bashan,
      for his steadfast love endures forever;
²¹ and gave their land as a heritage,
      for his steadfast love endures forever;
²² a heritage to Israel his servant,
      for his steadfast love endures forever.
²³ It is he who remembered us in our low estate,
      for his steadfast love endures forever;
²⁴ and rescued us from our foes,
      for his steadfast love endures forever;
²⁵ he who gives food to all flesh,
      for his steadfast love endures forever.

²⁶ Give thanks to the God of heaven,

    for his steadfast love endures forever.

John 3:16 – "For God so loved the world, that he gave his only Son, that whoever believes in him should not perish but have eternal life."

1 John 4:7-8 – ⁷ Beloved, let us love one another, for love is from God, and whoever loves has been born of God and knows God. ⁸ Anyone who does not love does not know God, because God is love.

God is love, which means that He is 100% love. God does not have or possess love; nor is love a percentage of Him. God is love entirely, infinitely, and perfectly. But what is love in God?

When the Bible says that God is love, God is telling us that He is Affection. But before creation, who did God have affection for? Himself. Only He existed before He chose to create. God perfectly loves Himself from eternity past. He is His own Beloved. And He is His Beloved in a way that no one else is.

Whoever loves, having known God's love through Christ, has been born of God. Having experienced God's love, by being born again through Christ, born from above, we love because He has loved us savingly. We know God in a way the world does not.

Psalm 63:3 – Because your steadfast love is better than life, my lips will praise you.

1 John 4:16 – So we have come to know and to believe the love that God has for us. God is love, and whoever abides in love abides in God, and God abides in him.

All Christians have come to know God, to truly understand His love. We all trust in the love that He has for us. It's His Divine love that calls us to salvation in Christ, and it's His love that keeps us saved.

God loves us, yet the world hates us, and our flesh hates us. Our sin wages war against us. Therefore, let us persevere in the faith, and live for God because He alone loves us perfectly.

God is love. Whoever lives in love, lives in God. And God lives in us.

Application

Since God is love and love is from God, lust is hate and must be from the devil. God loves us and has poured out His love on us in Christ, but the devil has only harmed us. How then could we embrace lust over love?

Like the devil, lust has done nothing good for us. It hates God, hates His design, hates us, and hates others. It only leads to death. Lust is contrary to God and His work in us.

Therefore, to lust is to be contrary to God, to be opposed to love.

Marching Orders: Thinking God's Thoughts After Him

Receive, believe, and live the truths you've read. Memorize and meditate on these truths today:

One Sentence to Shape Your Affections:

God is love, His design reflects this love, and all those born of Him live in love, which means that all that is contrary to Him or His design is hate; therefore, lust hates God, His design, me and others.

One Poem to Shape Your Affections:

Before the cosmos, earth, and sea,
God was there, loving Himself supremely.
He is His own Beloved, eternally true,
Loving Himself from the ages through.

I've come to know Him, in His love,
A love and knowledge the world dreams of.
I trust in His love that He has freely shown,
The love that calls me to His throne.

The world will hate, my flesh does fight,
And lust may cloud my inner light.
But if I abide in love, with God I'll stay,
He in me, and I in Him, with Christ always.

One Song to Shape Your Affections:

Add this song to your playlist, "O Great God."

On YouTube,
By Sovereign Grace Music (Written by Bob Kauflin)

https://www.youtube.com/watch?v=gOPbanJKWE8

[Due to copyright laws, I cannot include the lyrics here, but they are included in the above video.]

End with Prayer

Day 11

God is Triune / Lust is Selfish

Begin with Prayer

Scripture and Reflection

Isaiah 42:8, 11 – ⁸ I am the Lord; that is my name; my glory I give to no other, nor my praise to carved idols.
¹¹ For my own sake, for my own sake, I do it, for how should my name be profaned? My glory I will not give to another.

Matthew 28:19 – Go therefore and make disciples of all nations, baptizing them in the name of the Father and of the Son and of the Holy Spirit,

2 Corinthians 13:14 – The grace of the Lord Jesus Christ and the love of God and the fellowship of the Holy Spirit be with you all.

Jesus commands His disciples to make disciples of all nations, saying, "Baptize them in the Name," singular, but then lists three Persons: Father, Son, and Holy Spirit. God guards His glory, sharing it with no one else, yet He shares it with the Son and Holy Spirit. Why? Because these three Persons are one God, one Nature.

All that the Father is, the Son and Holy Spirit are as well. Their distinction lies not in their Nature but their relational order: The Father eternally begets the Son, the Son is eternally begotten of the Father, and the Holy Spirit proceeds from the Father and the Son. These three Persons are relationally distinct, logically distinct, yet one in being.

John 3:35 – The Father loves the Son and has given all things into his hand.

John 5:20 – For the Father loves the Son and shows him all that he himself is doing. And greater works than these will he show him, so that you may marvel.

John 17:20-23 –

> [20] "I do not ask for these only, but also for those who will believe in me through their word, [21] that they may all be one, just as you, Father, are in me, and I in you, that they also may be in us, so that the world may believe that you have sent me. [22] The glory that you have given me I have given to them, that they may be one even as we are one, [23] I in them and you in me, that they may become perfectly one, so that the world may know that you sent me and loved them even as you loved me."

The Father, Son, and Holy Spirit dwell in and with one another in unblemished community, perfectly one. In addition to loving themselves, they love one another without fail. They are one another's beloved.

From God flows unity and love into the hearts of Christians. Christ's bride must mirror this oneness and love. As the Trinity is united, so the church should stand, interconnected in unfailing affection for one another, from our hearts.

Application

When you lust, you turn from God's unity and love. Instead of seeking Him above yourself and striving to mirror His beauty in creation, you selfishly twist His gifts—your heart, soul, and mind—to crown lust your king, forsaking God's call to reflect His unity and love.

Lust wounds every bond you have: family, church, friends, and more. You cannot hold lust in your heart and be united and loving to your fellow image-bearers and fellow Christians (Prov 6:27-29). Lust, at its core, uses other people, without their knowledge and against their will, leavening your heart with selfishness, causing you to diminish others in all of your relationships.

God saved us so that we would shine forth His unity and love, yet lust reflects only the enemy's darkness, his perverse intent. If you cherish God's unity and love, if you adore the Father, Son, and Holy Spirit; if you treasure the local church; and delight in His word, how can lust find a home in your heart?

Marching Orders: Thinking God's Thoughts After Him

Receive, believe, and live the truths you've read. Memorize and meditate on these truths today:

One Sentence to Shape Your Affections:

There is one God who eternally exists in three distinct Persons: Father, Son, and Holy Spirit; the Father lovingly begets the Son; the Son is lovingly begotten from the Father; the Spirit lovingly proceeds from the Father and the Son; these three Persons are one Divine Nature; therefore, since lust is not from God, it does not give but selfishly takes of myself and others for sin.

One Poem to Shape Your Affections:

From ancient days, the faithful knew,
The triune God, infinite, true.
One God alone, eternal, vast,
Three Persons distinct, the First and Last.

All that the Father is in light,
The Son and Spirit are by right.
Their distinction lies in order's trace,
Not in their being, but their logical place.

The Father begets the Son always,
Eternal birth in timeless days.
The Holy Spirit proceeds from Father and Son,
Distinct in order as these Three are One.

The Trinity in loving harmony, my selfish lusts to mend,

So, I will reflect Him without end.

From the Father, Son, and Spirit's throne,

Let selflessness and love in me be sown.

One Song to Shape Your Affections:

Add this song to your playlist, "The Church's One Foundation."

On YouTube,

By Indelible Grace (Written by Samuel John Stone)

https://www.youtube.com/watch?v=1M4ykkY3yjY

1. The church's one foundation

Is Jesus Christ her Lord,

She is His new creation

By water and the Word.

From heaven He came and sought her

To be His holy bride;

With His own blood He bought her,

And for her life He died.

2. Elect from every nation,

Yet one over all the earth;

Her charter of salvation,

One Lord, one faith, one birth;

One holy Name she blesses,

Partakes one holy food,

And to one hope she presses,

With every grace endued.

3. Though with a scornful wonder

Men see her sore oppressed,

By schisms rent asunder,
By heresies distressed,
Yet saints their watch are keeping;
Their cry goes up, "How long?"
And soon the night of weeping
Shall be the morn of song.

4. The church shall never perish,
Her dear Lord to defend
To guide, sustain and cherish,
Is with her to the end
Though there be those that hate her,
And false sons in her pale
Against a foe or traitor,
She ever shall prevail

5. Mid toil and tribulation,
And tumult of her war,
She waits the consummation
Of peace forevermore;
'Til, with the vision glorious,
Her longing eyes are blessed,
And the great church victorious
Shall be the church at rest.

6. Yet she on earth hath union
With God the Three in One,
And mystic sweet communion
With those whose rest is won.
O happy ones and holy!
Lord, give us grace that we

Like them, the meek and lowly,
On high may dwell with Thee.[12]

End with Prayer

---

[12] "The Church's One Foundation," Hymnary, Accessed September 13, 2025, https://hymnary.org/text/the_churchs_one_foundation.

Day 12

God is Unchanging / Lust Cannot Satisfy

Begin with Prayer

Scripture and Reflection

Psalm 102:25-27 – 25 Of old you laid the foundation of the earth, and the heavens are the work of your hands. 26 They will perish, but you will remain; they will all wear out like a garment. You will change them like a robe, and they will pass away, 27 but you are the same, and your years have no end.

Malachi 3:6 – "For I the Lord do not change; therefore you, O children of Jacob, are not consumed."

James 1:17 – Every good gift and every perfect gift is from above, coming down from the Father of lights, with whom there is no variation or shadow due to change.

God is immutable or unchanging in His Divine Nature, His Godness. He eternally exists, beyond the bounds of time and space, preceding all creation. He created all things out of nothing. Self-existent and sovereign, He stands apart from His creation. The concept of "need" applies only to creatures, not to God, for He lacks nothing.

God does not change. Were He to change, He would change for the better or for the worse, both impossible, because perfection cannot be improved upon or diminished. He is constant, without any variation.

83

Numbers 23:19 – ¹⁹ God is not man, that he should lie, or a son of man, that he should change his mind. Has he said, and will he not do it? Or has he spoken, and will he not fulfill it?

Deuteronomy 7:6-11 –

> ⁶ "For you are a people holy to the Lord your God. The Lord your God has chosen you to be a people for his treasured possession, out of all the peoples who are on the face of the earth. ⁷ It was not because you were more in number than any other people that the Lord set his love on you and chose you, for you were the fewest of all peoples, ⁸ but it is because the Lord loves you and is keeping the oath that he swore to your fathers, that the Lord has brought you out with a mighty hand and redeemed you from the house of slavery, from the hand of Pharaoh king of Egypt. ⁹ Know therefore that the Lord your God is God, the faithful God who keeps covenant and steadfast love with those who love him and keep his commandments, to a thousand generations, ¹⁰ and repays to their face those who hate him, by destroying them. He will not be slack with one who hates him. He will repay him to his face. ¹¹ You shall therefore be careful to do the commandment and the statutes and the rules that I command you today."

Hebrews 6:18b – …it is impossible for God to lie…

Not only is God's Nature unchanging, He's also unchanging in His commitments. When God says He will do something, He will surely do it, for He cannot do otherwise. God cannot lie. He is forever faithful.

Application

Lust, on the other hand, deceives by enticing you to trust in what cannot satisfy. Its ever-shifting nature ensures it leaves you empty and hollow, proven by its constant luring, once is never enough. This cycle reveals its worthless value; it never delivers what it promises, nor can it.

You were created to be satisfied in God alone (Deut 5:6-15; Matt 22:37-38), as the first four commandments and the greatest commandment teach us. No lust, or any other sin, can ever satisfy your needs, wants, or desires, because you were created for God's glory.

Unlike God, who is faithful and true, lust reflects its father the devil; promising joy, satisfaction, and life, yet delivering only sorrow, disappointment, and death. Lust is a liar by nature, incapable of truth. Do not be deceived by it.

Today, will you give yourself to lust, which cannot satisfy? Or will you give yourself to God who can satisfy you today, tomorrow, and forever?

Marching Orders: Thinking God's Thoughts After Him

Receive, believe, and live the truths you've read. Memorize and meditate on these truths today:

One Sentence to Shape Your Affections:

God is unchanging, it's what He is; and He can never break His commitments, it's who He is, but lust always changes and can never satisfy me.

One Poem to Shape Your Affections:

God, the unchanging One, forever whole,
Self-existent, sovereign, and in control.
No need He has, and no lack to find,
No change for better or worse, not even His mind.

His promises, true, His decrees are certain,
With no veil of deceit, and no shadowing curtain.
But lust deceives, and is ever changing,
Leading its followers to the end of a noose, hanging.

One Song to Shape Your Affections:

Add this song to your playlist, "Great is Thy Faithfulness."

On YouTube,

By Hymns of Grace (Written by Thomas O. Chisholm)

https://www.youtube.com/watch?v=4Zj6EwlL9E0

1. Great is thy faithfulness, O God, my Father;
There is no shadow of turning with thee.
Thou changest not, thy compassions, they fail not;
As thou hast been, thou forever wilt be.

Refrain: Great is thy faithfulness,
Great is thy faithfulness,
Morning by morning new mercies I see.
All I have needed thy hand hast provided;
Great is thy faithfulness,
Lord unto me.

2. Summer and winter and springtime and harvest,
Sun, moon, and stars in their courses above
Join with all nature in manifold witness
To thy great faithfulness, mercy, and love.

3. Pardon for sin and a peace that endureth,
Thine own dear presence to cheer and to guide;
Strength for today and bright hope for tomorrow,
Blessings all mine and ten thousand beside.[13]

End with Prayer

---

[13] "Great is Thy Faithfulness," Hymnary, Accessed September 13, 2025,
https://hymnary.org/text/great_is_thy_faithfulness_o_god_my_fathe.

Day 13

Jesus is Truly God and Truly Man / Lust Images Satan

Begin with Prayer

Scripture and Reflection

Matthew 1:23 – "Behold, the virgin shall conceive and bear a son, and they shall call his name Immanuel" (which means, God with us).

Matthew 3:1-3 – "In those days John the Baptist came preaching in the wilderness of Judea, 2 "Repent, for the kingdom of heaven is at hand." 3 For this is he who was spoken of by the prophet Isaiah when he said, "The voice of one crying in the wilderness: 'Prepare the way of the Lord; make his paths straight'" [Isaiah 40:3].

Matthew 11:27 – "All things have been handed over to me by my Father, and no one knows the Son except the Father, and no one knows the Father except the Son and anyone to whom the Son chooses to reveal him."

Matthew 28:20b – "And behold, I am with you always, to the end of the age."

Jesus is truly God, YHWH the Son, with us. John the Baptist, fulfilling Isaiah's prophecy, prepared the way for YHWH, who is Jesus. Only Jesus truly knows His Father because He is one with Him. Likewise, only those whom Jesus chooses to reveal the Father will know Him as well.

Matthew 4:2 – And after fasting forty days and forty nights, he [Jesus] was hungry.

Matthew 24:36 – "But concerning that day and hour no one knows, not even the angels of heaven, nor the Son, but the Father only."

Matthew 26:38 – Then he said to them, "My soul is very sorrowful, even to death; remain here, and watch with me."

Matthew 26:39 – And going a little farther he fell on his face and prayed, saying, "My Father, if it be possible, let this cup pass from me; nevertheless, not as I will, but as you will."

Luke 2:7 – And she gave birth to her firstborn son and wrapped him in swaddling cloths and laid him in a manger, because there was no place for them in the inn.

Luke 23:46 – Then Jesus, calling out with a loud voice, said, "Father, into your hands I commit my spirit!" And having said this he breathed his last.

Colossians 1:15 – He is the image of the invisible God, the firstborn of all creation.

Not only is Jesus truly God, but He is also truly Man. Conceived by the Holy Spirit in Mary's womb, the Second Person of the Trinity, the Divine Son, united Himself to a human nature. He has a human will, soul, and body, and lived a truly human life: hungering, thirsting, learning, suffering, and dying. He is the perfect image of the invisible God.

Jesus is God the Son Incarnate; the Second Person of the Trinity united to His Divine Nature and human nature. He is truly God and truly Man. His two natures are united and distinct in His Divine Person without mixture or separation. Because Jesus is God the Son, He is holy from conception and lives forever in perfect holiness.

Romans 8:28-30 –
28 And we know that for those who love God all things work together for good, for those who are called according to his purpose. 29 For those whom

88

he foreknew he also predestined to be conformed to the image of his Son, in order that he might be the firstborn among many brothers. [30] And those whom he predestined he also called, and those whom he called he also justified, and those whom he justified he also glorified.

God has predestined His church to be conformed to the image of His Son. Born of Adam, we've been born again of Jesus, the Second Adam (John 3:1-8). God the Son united Himself to humanity so that our humanity would become like His own.

Application

When you lust, you live as though God saved you to conform you to the devil's image rather than the image of His Son. Lust reflects the evil one, yet you no longer belong to him.

As a Christian, foreknown and predestined by God to reflect Christ perfectly (Rom 8:29), our lust lies about Jesus, implying that God's Son lusts. God has tied His name to us, and He is shaping us into the likeness of the greatest name among men, Jesus Christ (Phil 2:9). Through rebirth, God calls us to embody Christ's likeness.

United to Jesus by the Holy Spirit, you are one with God the Son Incarnate. To lust is to take what is joined to Him and, in your heart, unite it with evil (1 Cor 6:12-20). You are too precious for that; you belong to Christ.

Believing that Christ is God the Son Incarnate and that we are united to Him by the Holy Spirit, by grace through faith in Christ, should drive us to turn from lust and turn to Christ and His ethics. We are better than lust, but do you believe these truths? If so, then live them.

Marching Orders: Thinking God's Thoughts After Him

Receive, Believe, and live the truths you've read. Memorize and meditate on these truths today:

One Sentence to Shape Your Affections:

Jesus, truly God and truly Man, is united to two natures, union without mixture and distinction without separation, in His Divine Person; and all Christians are being conformed to His perfect image; while lust rebels against God, seeking to conform me to Satan's image.

One Poem to Shape Your Affections:

Jesus, YHWH the Son, with me dwells,
His way, paved by the Baptist, hear Isaiah's voice.
Sole Knower of the Father's boundless wells,
He shares that spring only by sovereign choice.

Man and God, one Divine Person in Mary's frame,
Holy-Spirit-wrought, the Word took breath,
Felt my thirst and hunger, and bore my shame,
Mirroring God through life, yet obedient to death.

Two Natures united in God the Son,
One truly human, one truly Divine,
Unmixed, yet distinct without separation,
Natures different, but no rift, no severing line.

Me, from Adam's seed but in Christ born again,
Predestined by the Father's will, in Christ to share.
Lustful humanity, chosen by God, never to sin,
To reflect Him, His holy likeness, forever to wear.

One Song to Shape Your Affections:

Add this song to your playlist, "Immovable Our Hope Remains."

On YouTube,
By Sovereign Grace Music (Written by Augustus Toplady)

https://www.youtube.com/watch?v=02cdShYExIo

[Due to copyright laws, I cannot include the lyrics here, but they are included in the above video.]

End with Prayer

Day 14

Jesus is the Seed of the Woman, of Noah / Lust is the Seed of Satan

Begin with Prayer

Scripture and Reflection

Genesis 1:26-28 –

> [26] Then God said, "Let us make man in our image, after our likeness. And let them have dominion over the fish of the sea and over the birds of the heavens and over the livestock and over all the earth and over every creeping thing that creeps on the earth." [27] So God created man in his own image, in the image of God he created him; male and female he created them. [28] And God blessed them. And God said to them, "Be fruitful and multiply and fill the earth and subdue it, and have dominion over the fish of the sea and over the birds of the heavens and over every living thing that moves on the earth."

Genesis 3:15 – "I will put enmity between you and the woman, and between your offspring and her offspring; he shall bruise your head, and you shall bruise his heel."

God created mankind, male and female, in His image to reflect Him in at least four distinct ways:

1) Morally.
2) Thinking and reasoning.

3) Relationships.

4) Dominion over creation.

But mankind sinned against God, marring His image and mirroring the evil one through sin instead (Gen 3).

Yet, God showed mercy and grace to mankind, proclaiming the gospel in Genesis 3:15. After the serpent sinned in tempting Adam and Eve, and after they sinned by desiring and partaking of the forbidden tree, God said He would put hostility between the serpent's offspring and the woman's. From the Garden of Eden forward throughout human history, these seeds would war, but the woman's Seed would crush the serpent's head, though His heel would be bruised.

Genesis 6:5-8 –

5 The Lord saw that the wickedness of man was great in the earth, and that every intention of the thoughts of his heart was only evil continually. 6 And the Lord regretted that he had made man on the earth, and it grieved him to his heart. 7 So the Lord said, "I will blot out man whom I have created from the face of the land, man and animals and creeping things and birds of the heavens, for I am sorry that I have made them." 8 But Noah found favor in the eyes of the Lord.

Genesis 9:1-7 –

And God blessed Noah and his sons and said to them, "Be fruitful and multiply and fill the earth. 2 The fear of you and the dread of you shall be upon every beast of the earth and upon every bird of the heavens, upon everything that creeps on the ground and all the fish of the sea. Into your hand they are delivered. 3 Every moving thing that lives shall be food for you. And as I gave you the green plants, I give you everything. 4 But you shall not eat flesh with its life, that is, its blood. 5 And for your lifeblood I will require a reckoning: from every beast I will require it and from man. From his fellow man I will require a reckoning for the life of man. 6 'Whoever sheds the blood of man, by man shall his blood be shed, for God made man in his own image.

⁷ And you, be fruitful and multiply, increase greatly on the earth and multiply in it.'"

From Adam to Noah, mankind increased in wickedness, to where his entire intent was evil continually, but Noah found grace in God's sight. God judged mankind, flooding the entire earth, killing all but Noah, his wife, and their sons—Shem, Ham, and Japheth—and their wives. Through a covenant (Gen 6:18), God commanded Noah to build an ark, sheltering pairs of every creature—animal, bird, and creeping thing—along with provisions for all.

Genesis 9:20-27 –

> ²⁰ Noah began to be a man of the soil, and he planted a vineyard. ²¹ He drank of the wine and became drunk and lay uncovered in his tent. ²² And Ham, the father of Canaan, saw the nakedness of his father and told his two brothers outside. ²³ Then Shem and Japheth took a garment, laid it on both their shoulders, and walked backward and covered the nakedness of their father. Their faces were turned backward, and they did not see their father's nakedness. ²⁴ When Noah awoke from his wine and knew what his youngest son had done to him, ²⁵ he said, "Cursed be Canaan; a servant of servants shall he be to his brothers." ²⁶ He also said, "Blessed be the Lord, the God of Shem; and let Canaan be his servant. ²⁷ May God enlarge Japheth, and let him dwell in the tents of Shem, and let Canaan be his servant."

God wiped out all of humanity except for Noah and his family, treating Noah as a new Adam. From Noah's seed would come the One who would crush the serpent's head (Gen 3:15), though the serpent's seed slipped aboard through Ham, who sinned against his father, resulting in him and Canaan being cursed by Noah. Yet, Noah blessed his other sons, Shem and Japheth, because they demonstrated their faith in God, believing that Noah should be treated according to God's favor of him as a new Adam. Shem was especially blessed as the firstborn, his lineage bearing Jesus Christ, the promised Seed of the woman (Luke 3:23-38).

Application

When you lust, you reflect the serpent not God, whose image you were designed to mirror. Because God designed you, you are too good to lust; a truth rooted in creation.

Yet, there's an even greater reason why you shouldn't lust: as a Christian, reborn in Christ (John 3:1-8), you have been born again in the likeness of the Seed of the woman and Noah, Jesus Himself. Noah longed for Him, not the fleeting lust that Ham chased.

United to Jesus Christ through the Holy Spirit, how can you echo Satan and Ham? Twice claimed, by creation and rebirth, you belong to God, not the serpent. Live today as who you are in Him.

Marching Orders: Thinking God's Thoughts After Him

Receive, Believe, and live the truths you've read. Memorize and meditate on these truths today:

One Sentence to Shape Your Affections:

Jesus Christ came to crush the serpent's head, fulfilling the types and shadows of Adam and Noah; while lust seeks to repeat the lives of Cain and all those destroyed in the flood.

One Poem to Shape Your Affections:

In His image, God created man and wife,
To mirror His ways through mortal life.
Reflecting His morality, reason, love, and reign,
Yet sin stained all, spreading the serpent's fame.

But God spoke hope in Eden's dark shade,
The woman would give birth; the serpent would be slayed.
His heel pierced through, death would be His cost,

Legion would laugh, but redemption's hope would not be lost.

Man's evil swelled, till God's flood swept through,
Yet grace upheld Noah, Shem, and Japheth, faithful and true.
A new Adam stood, his kin on the ark aboard,
But sin still lurked in Ham's heart, he and the serpent in accord.

By God's design, from Shem's line, the Christ would spring,
The serpent's doom laid bare at the feet of salvation's King.
At Eden's lustful breach, a promise was given,
And from an angel I hear, "He is not here, for He has risen."

One Song to Shape Your Affections:

Add this song to your playlist, "Deceived by Subtle Snares of Hell."

On YouTube,
Song by SSNGAI (Written by Isaac Watts)

https://www.youtube.com/watch?v=xHg0h7Et-jg

1. Deceived by subtle snares of hell,
Adam, our head, our father, fell;
When Satan, in the serpent hid,
Proposed the fruit that God forbid.

2. Death was the threat'ning: death began
To take possession of the man
His unborn race received the wound,
And heavy curses smote the ground.

3. But Satan found a worse reward;
Thus saith the vengeance of the Lord

"Let everlasting hatred be
Betwixt the woman's seed and thee.

4. "The woman's seed shall be my Son;
He shall destroy what thou hast done;
Shall break thy head, and only feel
Thy malice raging at his heel."

5. He spake; and bid four thousand years
Roll on; at length his Son appears;
Angels with joy descend to earth,
And sing the young Redeemer's birth.

6. Lo, by the sons of hell he dies;
But as he hung 'twixt earth and skies,
He gave their prince a fatal blow,
And triumphed o'er the powers below.[14]

End with Prayer

---

[14] "The Fall and Recovery of Man; or, Christ and Satan at Enmity," Hymnary, Accessed September 13, 2025, https://hymnary.org/text/deceived_by_subtle_snares_of_hell.

Day 15

Jesus is the Seed of the Woman, of Abraham / Lust is the Seed of Satan

Begin with Prayer

Scripture and Reflection

Genesis 1:27 – So, God created man in his own image, in the image of God he created him; male and female he created them.

Genesis 3:15 – "I will put enmity between you and the woman, and between your offspring and her offspring; he shall bruise your head, and you shall bruise his heel."

The true humanity of Christ is essential because Adam, a true human, caused the Fall of all mankind into sin. Only mankind is God's image-bearers, male and female, not angels or animals. It was a man who led us into sin, and so it must be a Man who redeems us out of it.

In Genesis 3:15, God tells the serpent that He will put enmity between his seed and the woman's Seed. The serpent will bruise His heel, but the woman's Seed will crush his head. Jesus is that promised Seed. And what is a seed of a woman? By the order of creation, it is her offspring, a true human being. The coming Messiah had to be truly Man.

Genesis 17:4-8 –

> 4 "Behold, my covenant is with you, and you shall be the father of a multitude of nations. 5 No longer shall your name be called Abram, but your name shall be Abraham, for I have made you the father of a multitude of nations. 6 I will make you exceedingly fruitful, and I will make you into nations, and kings shall come from you. 7 And I will establish my covenant between me and you and your offspring after you throughout their generations for an everlasting covenant, to be God to you and to your offspring after you. 8 And I will give to you and to your offspring after you the land of your sojournings, all the land of Canaan, for an everlasting possession, and I will be their God."

Genesis 21:12 – But God said to Abraham, "Be not displeased because of the boy and because of your slave woman. Whatever Sarah says to you, do as she tells you, for through Isaac shall your offspring be named."

Genesis 22:17-18 – "17 I will surely bless you, and I will surely multiply your offspring as the stars of heaven and as the sand that is on the seashore. And your offspring shall possess the gate of his enemies, 18 and in your offspring shall all the nations of the earth be blessed, because you have obeyed my voice."

Matthew 1:1 – The book of the genealogy of Jesus Christ, the son of David, the son of Abraham.

Galatians 3:16 – Now the promises were made to Abraham and to his offspring. It does not say, "And to offsprings," referring to many, but referring to one, "And to your offspring," who is Christ.

God's prophecy to Abraham about his offspring pointed to the coming of Jesus Christ from Abraham's lineage. Through Christ, all the nations of the earth would be blessed (Gen 22:17-18). In Genesis 21:12, God tells Abraham "Through Isaac shall your offspring be named."

Isaac is a single individual, who was Abraham's son of promise. Likewise, Isaac's son, Jacob, not his son Esau, was his son of promise. And, out of the twelve tribes of Jacob (later named Israel), only Judah was the son of promise, whose lineage would produce the Messiah (Gen 49:8-12).

From the Garden to Noah to Abraham, the trajectory of God's prophecy has been through one chosen "Seed," a singular son in each generation, culminating in Jesus Christ. He is the ultimate Seed of the woman (Gen 3:15), the Seed of Abraham, and the Son of God, in whom the promise is fully realized.

Imagine reading the Bible from Genesis forward for the first time: you'd be on the edge of your seat looking for the Seed of the woman. You'd think it was Noah, then Abraham, or David, until they sinned. Then, when you got to Jesus Christ, you would realize that He is the long-awaited Seed of the Woman, of Abraham.

Application

When you lust, you chase a fleeting thrill, not the promise Abraham and the patriarchs longed for, but the twisted desire the serpent craved when he walked into Eden. All that plagues you, me, and humanity traces back to his envy.

When you lust, you surrender to a lineage still within you that has already been crucified with Christ. That part of you, your flesh, is dead and your debt has been paid in full. Do not walk in death.

You belong to Christ's line, reborn through Him; so live like it. Lust is not Christ's way, and it shouldn't be yours. When you sin, repent. Turn to Abraham's Offspring, Jesus Christ, for forgiveness and the strength to live for His glory.

The evil one could not stop the Seed of the woman from being born. He could not stop you from being born again either. And he can't derail your eternal sanctification.

Rise up. Embrace what the Lord has done, and is doing, in your heart. Live for Christ.

Marching Orders: Thinking God's Thoughts After Him

Receive, believe, and live the truths you've read. Memorize and meditate on these truths today:

One Sentence to Shape Your Affections:

Jesus Christ, the Seed of the woman, of Abraham, came to crush the serpent's head, fulfilling all the Old Testament types and shadows; while lust seeks to repeat the lives of all those who rejected YHWH in history.

One Poem to Shape Your Affections:

God's image shines in mankind alone,
Not animal nor angel claims this throne.
From dust to Adam, a human tale,
True man chose sin, and all men fell.

A man brought death, a Man must save,
Only the woman's Seed, pure and brave.
Her offspring crushes the serpent's head,
Though bruised, He triumphs over the dead.

Through Abraham, the promise flows,
A single line where blessing grows.
Isaac born, then Jacob true,
In Judah's line, the King breaks through.

From Eden's Fall to Zion's Son,
One chosen Seed, the Holy One.
Abraham stumbles, David sins,
Yet their Son, my heart, He mends.

Trace the Seed with a steadfast gaze,
A thread of grace through a shadowed maze.

At last He comes, the woman's Seed,
Abraham's joy, the luster's need.

One Song to Shape Your Affections:

Add this song to your playlist, "Come Thou Long Expected Jesus."

On YouTube,
By Sandra McCracken & Derek Webb (Written by Charles Wesley)

https://www.youtube.com/watch?v=Djc_cT6cwlU

1. Come Thou long-expected Jesus
Born to set Thy people free;
From our fears and sins release us,
Let us find our rest in Thee.
Israel's strength and consolation,
Hope of all the saints Thou art;
Dear desire of every nation,
Joy of every longing heart.

2. Born Thy people to deliver,
Born a child and yet a King,
Born to reign in us forever,
Now Thy gracious kingdom bring.
By Thine own eternal Spirit
Rule in all our hearts alone;
By Thine all sufficient merit,
Raise us to Thy glorious throne.[15]

End with Prayer

---

[15] "Come, Thou Long Expected Jesus," Hymnary, Accessed September 13, 2025,
https://hymnary.org/text/come_thou_long_expected_jesus_born_to.

Day 16

Jesus is the Seed of the Woman, of Israel, of David / Lust is the Seed of Satan

Begin with Prayer

Scripture and Reflection

Genesis 3:15 – "I will put enmity between you and the woman, and between your offspring and her offspring; he shall bruise your head, and you shall bruise his heel."

In Genesis 3:15, God prophesied that there would be two peoples, Satan's offspring and the woman's Seed, locked in conflict throughout history until the woman's Seed crushes the serpent's head. Since Eden, humanity has split into the devil's kin and God's own people. The divide was evident in Noah, Shem, and Japheth, versus Ham (Day 14), and in Abraham set against his neighboring nations (Day 15). Now, we'll see it unfold with Israel and David, God's sons, facing the Gentiles.

Galatians 3:16 – Now the promises were made to Abraham and to his offspring. It does not say, "And to offsprings," referring to many, but referring to one, "And to your offspring," who is Christ.

Matthew 2:13-15 –

13 Now when they had departed, behold, an angel of the Lord appeared to Joseph in a dream and said, "Rise, take the child and his mother, and flee to Egypt, and remain there until I tell you, for Herod is about to search for the child, to destroy him." 14 And he rose and took the child and his mother by night and departed to Egypt 15 and remained there until the death of Herod. This was to fulfill what the Lord had spoken by the prophet, "Out of Egypt I called my son" [Hosea 11:1].

Hosea 11:1 – When Israel was a child, I loved him, and out of Egypt I called my son.

Israel was enslaved in Egypt for four hundred years. The prophet Hosea reveals that from this Gentile nation, God called His son (Hosea 11:1). Israel was God's son for the purpose of producing and pointing to God's true Son, the Seed of the woman, Jesus Christ. And Matthew said Hosea 11:1 was ultimately about Jesus, when he, Joseph, and Mary had to flee King Herod, because he sought to kill Jesus. Warned by an angel, they sought refuge in Egypt, returning to Nazareth in Israel after Herod's death (Matt 2:16-23).

2 Samuel 7:16 – And your [David] house and your kingdom shall be made sure forever before me. Your throne shall be established forever.

Isaiah 55:1-3 –

"Come, everyone who thirsts, come to the waters; and he who has no money, come, buy and eat! Come, buy wine and milk without money and without price. 2 Why do you spend your money for that which is not bread, and your labor for that which does not satisfy? Listen diligently to me, and eat what is good, and delight yourselves in rich food. 3 Incline your ear, and come to me; hear, that your soul may live; and I will make with you an everlasting covenant, my steadfast, sure love for David."

Jeremiah 33:14-16 –

> [14] "Behold, the days are coming, declares the Lord, when I will fulfill the promise I made to the house of Israel and the house of Judah. [15] In those days and at that time I will cause a righteous Branch to spring up for David, and he shall execute justice and righteousness in the land. [16] In those days Judah will be saved, and Jerusalem will dwell securely. And this is the name by which it will be called: 'The Lord is our righteousness.'"

Ezekiel 34:23-24 – [23] And I will set up over them one shepherd, my servant David, and he shall feed them: he shall feed them and be their shepherd. [24] And I, the Lord, will be their God, and my servant David shall be prince among them. I am the Lord; I have spoken.

Matthew 22:41-46 –

> [41] Now while the Pharisees were gathered together, Jesus asked them a question, [42] saying, "What do you think about the Christ? Whose son is he?" They said to him, "The son of David." [43] He said to them, "How is it then that David, in the Spirit, calls him Lord, saying, [44] "'The Lord said to my Lord, "Sit at my right hand, until I put your enemies under your feet"' [Ps 110:1]? [45] If then David calls him Lord, how is he his son?" [46] And no one was able to answer him a word, nor from that day did anyone dare to ask him any more questions.

Luke 1:31-33 – [31] "And behold, you will conceive in your womb and bear a son, and you shall call his name Jesus. [32] He will be great and will be called the Son of the Most High. And the Lord God will give to him the throne of his father David, [33] and he will reign over the house of Jacob forever, and of his kingdom there will be no end."

David was Israel's greatest and godliest king. God established his throne forever, saying that his Son would rule without end. Yet, David called his Son "Lord" in Psalm 110:1. Jesus points to this verse to teach that He is God the Son, David's greater Son that he called Lord, and the rightful heir to David's eternal throne (Matt 22:41-46).

Application

When you lust, though you're a son of God through your union with *the* Son of God, you act as if you're a son of the devil still. Israel's ultimate purpose was fulfilled in Christ. The faithful Israelites longed for Jesus, not for the fleeting lusts you chase.

Moreover, lust aligns you with the devil's fleeting throne, soon to perish forever (John 16:11). But God established David's throne forever. As a Christian, you are Christ's bride (2 Cor 11:2; Eph 5:25-32), united with the King of kings, seated "with Him in the heavenly places" (Eph 2:1-10).

In Christ, you are eternal royalty, too holy to lust.

Marching Orders: Thinking God's Thoughts After Him

Receive, Believe, and live the truths you've read. Memorize and meditate on these truths today:

One Sentence to Shape Your Affections:

Jesus Christ is the Seed of the woman, of Israel, of David, God's true Son, reigning on David's eternal throne forever; while lust is the seed of Satan, of the Canaanites, of the Philistines.

One Poem to Shape Your Affections:

From Eden's curse, history would unfold,
Two lines of seed, as God foretold:
The serpent's brood, the woman's kin,
A war the Sinless One would win.

God's chosen people clash with rebel heart,
Noah and Shem, and Ham apart.
Abraham stood against the nations bold,

And Israel was born from prophecies of old.

Hosea's call in Matthew rings,
From Gentile land, the Son of God springs.
Fleeing Herod's cruel blade,
In Egypt's shade, His refuge was made.

From death's dark tomb, Christ rose, a King so grand,
To reign on David's throne by God's command.
God the Son, victory won, lust's crushing has begun,
Jesus to soon return, to bring His kingdom, under the Son.

One Song to Shape Your Affections:

Add this song to your playlist, "O Come, O Come, Emmanuel."

On YouTube,
By Sovereign Grace Music (Verses 1-2 translated by John Mason Neale)

https://www.youtube.com/watch?v=2JpvW9FU_Rg

1. O come, O come, Emmanuel
And ransom captive Israel
That mourns in lonely exile here
Until the Son of God appear

Refrain: Rejoice! Rejoice! Emmanuel
Shall come to thee, O Israel

2. O come, Thou, Dayspring from on high
And cause Thy light on us to rise
Disperse the gloomy clouds of night
And death's dark shadow put to flight

[Due to copyright laws, I cannot include verses 3-5 here, but they are included in the above video.]

End with Prayer

Day 17

Jesus is the True Prophet / Lust is a False Prophet

Begin with Prayer

Scripture and Reflection

Deuteronomy 18:15-19 –

> 15 "The Lord your God will raise up for you a prophet like me from among you, from your brothers—it is to him you shall listen— 16 just as you desired of the Lord your God at Horeb on the day of the assembly, when you said, 'Let me not hear again the voice of the Lord my God or see this great fire any more, lest I die.' 17 And the Lord said to me, 'They are right in what they have spoken. 18 I will raise up for them a prophet like you from among their brothers. And I will put my words in his mouth, and he shall speak to them all that I command him. 19 And whoever will not listen to my words that he shall speak in my name, I myself will require it of him."

Deuteronomy 34:10-12 –

> 10 And there has not arisen a prophet since in Israel like Moses, whom the Lord knew face to face, 11 none like him for all the signs and the wonders that the Lord sent him to do in the land of Egypt, to Pharaoh and to all his servants and to all his land, 12 and for all the mighty power and all the great deeds of terror that Moses did in the sight of all Israel.

Matthew 21:10-11 – [10] And when he entered Jerusalem, the whole city was stirred up, saying, "Who is this?" [11] And the crowds said, "This is the prophet Jesus, from Nazareth of Galilee."

A prophet speaks on behalf of God to the people. Moses fulfilled this role. Matthew tells us in his Gospel that Jesus is God's Prophet, for the people said so. And God publicly identified Jesus as the Prophet Moses spoke of by directing His life to parallel Moses' life:

1. Jesus' birth was like Moses' birth:

> Herod sought to kill Jesus (Matt 2:13).
> Pharaoh sought to kill Moses (Ex 1:10, 16).

> Jesus was saved by fleeing to Egypt (Matt 2:13).
> Moses was saved by becoming a son of Egypt (Ex 2:1-10).

2. Jesus' Sermon on the Mount was similar to Moses' experience on Mount Sinai:

> Jesus ascended the mountain (Matt 5:1).
> Moses ascended Mount Sinai (Ex 24; 34).

> Jesus went up to preach the law authoritatively (Matt 5).
> Moses went up to receive the law (Ex 24; 34).[16]

3. Jesus' transfiguration was like Moses' transfiguration:

> Jesus went up on a high mountain (Matt 17:1).
> Moses went up on a high mountain (Ex 24:12, 15-18; 34:2-3).

> After six days, Jesus went up the mountain (Matt 17:1).
> The cloud covered Mount Sinai for six days (Ex 24:16).

> Jesus brought three people with Him: Peter, James, and John (Matt 17:1).

---

[16] Wayne S. Baxter, "Mosaic Imagery In The Gospel Of Matthew," *Trinity Journal* 20:1 (Spring 1999): 69-83.

Moses brought three people with him: Aaron, Nadab, and Abihu (Ex 24:1).

Jesus' face shone like the sun (Matt 17:2).
Moses' face shone like the sun (Ex 34:29-30, 35).

A cloud covered the mountain (Matt 17:5).
A cloud covered Mount Sinai (Ex 24:15-16).

YHWH spoke from the cloud (Matt 17:5).
YHWH spoke from the cloud (Ex 24:16).

The disciples were terrified (Matt 17:6).
Israel was terrified when they saw Moses' face (Ex 34:30).[17]

Jesus is the Prophet of God, the One who fulfills all the other prophets. He is the One that Moses longed for. As God the Father said from the cloud when Christ was transfigured, "This is my beloved Son, with whom I am well pleased; listen to him" (Matt 17:5). We are called by God to trust, listen to, and follow Christ as the ultimate Prophet who speaks God's word.

Application

Jesus is the great Prophet that fulfills all the other prophets. His voice offers life, peace, freedom, and truth. Will you listen to Him?

When you lust, you ignore Jesus. Lust is a false prophet that whispers the devil's ancient lie: "You will not surely die" (Gen 3:4). Yet, it chains your heart to the flesh, pulling you from fellowship and happiness in God. It promises pleasure but only delivers pain and death. Countless lives have been ensnared by its false promises; and billions have been taken to hell because of it, but Jesus offers the abundant life that is eternal.

---

[17] Patrick Schreiner, "Matthew's Gospel as You've Never Read it Before," September 6, 2019, https://www.thegospelcoalition.org/article/matthew-gospel-never-read-before/.

Choose life. Jesus, the true Prophet, who died and rose from the dead for you, calls you out of your lust to repent and believe in Him and to live His commands. Turn from sin, trust His forgiveness, submit to Him, and let His words reform your heart into His likeness. Get up and live for Him from your heart, because He not only calls you to life but empowers you by His Holy Spirit to live fully from your heart for Him.

Marching Orders: Thinking God's Thoughts After Him

Receive, believe, and live the truths you've read. Memorize and meditate on these truths today:

One Sentence to Shape Your Affections:

Jesus, the eternal true Prophet prophesied by Moses, came to proclaim God's word to the world, while lust denies Jesus's words and morals.

One Poem to Shape Your Affections:

A prophet speaks God's word to men,
Moses lived that role back then.
Matthew unveils Christ the Prophet true,
Fulfilling what an elderly Moses knew.

Pharaoh's sword sought Moses' life,
Herod's rage brought Jesus strife.
Egypt hid them both from harm,
Saved by God's plan under Gentile arm.

Forty days, in the wilderness tried,
Yet, Jesus rejected the devil's pride.
Forty years, Israel roamed astray,
Tested and tempted in Moses' day.

Moses climbed to Sinai's height,
On that mount, the law brought to sight.
Jesus preached with power unfurled,
A forgotten law, explained to a waiting world.

Transfigured on a peak so grand,
Moses radiated by God's command.
Jesus shined, as if the sun's own kin,
From the cloud, God's voice exalted Him then.

Three men joined Moses, three too with Christ,
Clouds engulfed, and fear sufficed.
From the midst, God's voice rang clear,
"Listen to my Son! Prick up your ear!"

Moses longed for the woman's Seed, then Jesus came,
The True Prophet of endless fame.
God's beloved, the final call,
In Him, not lust, the prophets find their all.

One Song to Shape Your Affections:

Add this song to your playlist, "How Sweet the Name of Jesus Sounds."

On YouTube,
By Matthew Perryman Jones (Written by John Newton)

https://www.youtube.com/watch?v=w71CDub1W2k

1. How sweet the name of Jesus sounds
in a believer's ear!
It soothes our sorrows, heals our wounds,
and drives away our fear.

115

2. It makes the wounded spirit whole
and calms the troubled breast;
'tis manna to the hungry soul,
and to the weary, rest.

3. O Jesus, shepherd, guardian, friend,
my Prophet, Priest, and King,
my Lord, my Life, my Way, my End,
accept the praise I bring.

4. How weak the effort of my heart,
how cold my warmest thought;
but when I see you as you are,
I'll praise you as I ought.

5. Till then I would your love proclaim
with every fleeting breath;
and may the music of your name
refresh my soul in death.[18]

End with Prayer

.

[18] "How Sweet the Name of Jesus Sounds," Hymnary, Accessed September 13, 2025,
https://hymnary.org/text/how_sweet_the_name_of_jesus_sounds_in_a.

Day 18

Jesus is the True High Priest / Lust is a Worthless Priest

Begin with Prayer

Scripture and Reflection

<u>Leviticus 4:20</u> – Thus shall he do with the bull. As he did with the bull of the sin offering, so shall he do with this. And the priest shall make atonement for them, and they shall be forgiven.

<u>Leviticus 21:16-20</u> –

16 And the Lord spoke to Moses, saying, 17 "Speak to Aaron, saying, None of your offspring throughout their generations who has a blemish may approach to offer the bread of his God. 18 For no one who has a blemish shall draw near, a man blind or lame, or one who has a mutilated face or a limb too long, 19 or a man who has an injured foot or an injured hand, 20 or a hunchback or a dwarf or a man with a defect in his sight or an itching disease or scabs or crushed testicles."

<u>Matthew 9:1-8</u> –

And getting into a boat he crossed over and came to his own city. 2 And behold, some people brought to him a paralytic, lying on a bed. And when Jesus saw their faith, he said to the paralytic, "Take heart, my son; your sins are forgiven." 3 And behold, some of the scribes said to themselves, "This man is blaspheming." 4 But Jesus, knowing their thoughts, said, "Why do you think evil in your hearts? 5 For which is easier, to say, 'Your sins are forgiven,' or to say, 'Rise and walk'? 6 But that you may know that the Son of Man has authority on earth to forgive sins"—he then said to the paralytic—"Rise, pick up your bed and go home." 7 And he rose and went home. 8 When the crowds saw it, they were afraid, and they glorified God, who had given such authority to men.

In the Old Testament, God granted forgiveness through the Levitical priests, but they did not have the power or authority to forgive sins. They also were told to exclude the disabled and diseased as unclean. Jesus, however, is able to forgive sins and heal the disabled and diseased because He is God the Son in the flesh, the ultimate High Priest forever. He separates the clean and unclean by forgiving and saving them and making them clean eternally.

Leviticus 10:11 – "and you are to teach the people of Israel all the statutes that the Lord has spoken to them by Moses."

Matthew 5:27-28 – 27 "You have heard that it was said, 'You shall not commit adultery.' 28 But I say to you that everyone who looks at a woman with lustful intent has already committed adultery with her in his heart."

The Levitical priests taught the law to God's people. Jesus, in His Sermon on the Mount, corrected the Pharisees' false teaching by teaching the law correctly. And He also taught with a greater authority than Levitical priests. He went up on a high mountain but did not receive the law like Moses on Mount Sinai, and instead, taught the law with God's authority.

Leviticus 10:10 – You are to distinguish between the holy and the common, and between the unclean and the clean.

Matthew 25:31-34, 41, 46 –

31 "When the Son of Man comes in his glory, and all the angels with him, then he will sit on his glorious throne. 32 Before him will be gathered all the nations, and he will separate people one from another as a shepherd separates the sheep from the goats. 33 And he will place the sheep on his right, but the goats on the left. 34 Then the King will say to those on his right, 'Come, you who are blessed by my Father, inherit the kingdom prepared for you from the foundation of the world...

41 "Then he will say to those on his left, 'Depart from me, you cursed, into the eternal fire prepared for the devil and his angels...

46 And these will go away into eternal punishment, but the righteous into eternal life."

Levitical priests separated those who were clean from those who were unclean, according to the law. But Jesus separated the believers from the unbelievers. Even on the cross, before He died, He separated the believing thief from the unbelieving thief by being crucified between them. He led one of them to be saved and took Him to Paradise that day (Luke 23:39-43).

Leviticus 13:1-4 –

The Lord spoke to Moses and Aaron, saying, 2 "When a person has on the skin of his body a swelling or an eruption or a spot, and it turns into a case of leprous disease on the skin of his body, then he shall be brought to Aaron the priest or to one of his sons the priests, 3 and the priest shall examine the diseased area on the skin of his body. And if the hair in the diseased area has turned white and the disease appears to be deeper than the skin of his body, it is a case of leprous disease. When the priest has examined him, he shall pronounce him unclean."

Matthew 8:1-4 –

"When he came down from the mountain, great crowds followed him. 2 And behold, a leper came to him and knelt before him, saying, "Lord, if you will, you can make me clean." 3 And Jesus stretched out his hand and touched him, saying, "I will; be clean." And immediately his leprosy was cleansed. ⁴ And Jesus said to him, "See that you say nothing to anyone, but go, show yourself to the priest and offer the gift that Moses commanded, for a proof to them."

The Levitical priests were responsible for examining individuals for signs of leprosy and declared those afflicted as unclean. But Jesus, He cleansed the leper, making him clean instead of declaring him unclean. He then instructed the healed man to present himself to the High Priest, to fulfill the law, and to prove that Jesus is greater, the ultimate High Priest forever.

2 Chronicles 29:15 – They gathered their brothers and consecrated themselves and went in as the king had commanded, by the words of the Lord, to cleanse the house of the Lord.

Matthew 21:12-13 – ¹² And Jesus entered the temple and drove out all who sold and bought in the temple, and he overturned the tables of the money-changers and the seats of those who sold pigeons. ¹³ He said to them, "It is written, 'My house shall be called a house of prayer,' but you make it a den of robbers."

Romans 8:34 – Who is to condemn? Christ Jesus is the one who died—more than that, who was raised—who is at the right hand of God, who indeed is interceding for us.

Hebrews 7:25 – Consequently, he is able to save to the uttermost those who draw near to God through him, since he always lives to make intercession for them.

1 John 2:1 – My little children, I am writing these things to you so that you may not sin. But if anyone does sin, we have an advocate with the Father, Jesus Christ the righteous.

Under the leadership of King Ahaz, Judah declined in their devotion to and worship of YHWH. Ahaz promoted idolatry and neglected the temple. His son, King Hezekiah, led Judah to repent, opening and repairing the temple, and instructing the priests to purify themselves and the temple for worship. In contrast, Jesus, being sinless and requiring no purification, cleansed the temple by driving out the moneychangers, condemning their exploitation of His Father's house as a den of thieves. Jesus lives today, seated at His Father's right hand, always interceding for His church.[19]

Application

When you lust, you trust in something that puts a wedge between you and God. Yet Christ, as the perfect High Priest, intercedes for you with unfailing love (Rom 8:34; Heb 7:25; 1 John 2:1). Why would you give your affections to lust when it only harms you, and harms your relationship with God and others?

Lust leads you astray, teaching you a false law and gospel. It misguides your heart morally while offering you empty promises of the abundant life that it can never fulfill. It whispers, "You will be happy forever," as it leads you to the grave, and if possible, to hell.

Lust clouds your judgment rendering you unable to discern the difference between good and evil. To justify lust in your heart, you must call evil good and good evil. And if you're willing to lie to yourself in this way about lust, you will also lie to yourself about other sins.

You are the temple of God. Jesus has cleansed your temple, and resides in you through His Holy Spirit, but lust defiles you. Knowing this, how can you join God's temple to lust?

Marching Orders: Thinking God's Thoughts After Him

Receive, believe, and live the truths you've read. Memorize and meditate on these truths today:

---

[19] David Schrock, "5 Ways We See Jesus Serve as a Priest," Crossway, July 17, 2022, https://www.crossway.org/articles/5-ways-we-see-jesus-serve-as-a-priest/.

One Sentence to Shape Your Affections:

Jesus Christ is the ultimate High Priest, the fulfillment of all the priests who came before Him, interceding with His own death and righteousness for both believing Jew and Gentile before God; while lust cannot stand in God's presence and harms my relationship with God.

One Poem to Shape Your Affections:

God forgave through Levite rites, not their power,
The disabled, excluded from worship, unclean every hour.
Jesus, supreme High Priest, God's Son Divine,
Heals and forgives with power, His glory to shine.

God the Son on the Mount, taught with authority,
The law to fulfill, to set free from the Pharisee.
Priests marked the clean, the unclean set apart,
Jesus divided them by faith, discerning the heart.

Leprosy judged, priests marked the stain,
But Jesus cleansed the lepers, healing their pain.
Ahaz brought idols. Hezekiah and Levite, the temple renewed,
And Jesus cleansed the temple, a den of thieves subdued.

Pure, He cleansed what the lustful did defile,
He is the eternal High Priest, in Him is no guile.
Interceding for His people, His love remains and sustains,
Fulfilling all High Priests, with grace He forever reigns.

One Song to Shape Your Affections:

Add this song to your playlist, "Arise, My Soul, Arise."

On YouTube,
Song by Sovereign Grace Music (Written by Charles Wesley)

https://www.youtube.com/watch?v=fiHxEuL1dd0

1. Arise, my soul, arise; shake off thy guilty fears
The bleeding sacrifice in my behalf appears
Before the throne my surety stands
Before the throne my surety stands
My name is written on His hands

2. Five bleeding wounds He bears, received on Calvary
They pour effectual prayers; they strongly plead for me
"Forgive him, oh forgive," they cry
"Forgive him, oh forgive," they cry
"Nor let that ransomed sinner die!"

3. The Father hears Him pray, His dear Anointed One
He cannot turn away the presence of His Son
His Spirit answers to the blood
His Spirit answers to the blood
And tells me I am born of God

4. My God is reconciled; His pardoning voice I hear
He owns me for His child; I can no longer fear
With confidence I now draw nigh
With confidence I now draw nigh
And "Father, Abba, Father" cry[20]

End with Prayer

[20] "Arise, My Soul, Arise," Hymnary, Accessed September 13, 2025,
https://hymnary.org/text/arise_my_soul_arise_shake_off_thy_guilty.

Day 19

Jesus is the True King / Lust is an Unrighteous King

Begin with Prayer

Scripture and Reflection

2 Samuel 7:12-14 –

> 12 When your days are fulfilled and you lie down with your fathers, I will raise up your offspring after you, who shall come from your body, and I will establish his kingdom. 13 He shall build a house for my name, and I will establish the throne of his kingdom forever. 14 I will be to him a father, and he shall be to me a son.

God prophesied through the Prophet Nathan that there will be a son from David's line whose throne and kingdom will last forever.

Matthew 1:1-2 – The book of the genealogy of Jesus Christ, the son of David, the son of Abraham. 2 Abraham was the father of Isaac, and Isaac the father of Jacob, and Jacob the father of Judah and his brothers,

Matthew 1:6 – and Jesse the father of David the king. And David was the father of Solomon by the wife of Uriah,

Matthew 1:16 – and Jacob the father of Joseph the husband of Mary, of whom Jesus was born, who is called Christ.

Matthew's Gospel traces Jesus' lineage through Abraham and David to Joseph, His earthly father. Though Joseph was not Jesus' biological father, Joseph included Jesus in his household, fulfilling the prophecies of a son to be born of Abraham and David, since Joseph was their descendant.

Luke 3:23 – "Jesus, when he began his ministry, was about thirty years of age, being the son (as was supposed) of Joseph, the son of Heli,"

Luke 3:31 – the son of Melea, the son of Menna, the son of Mattatha, the son of Nathan, the son of David,

Luke 3:34 – the son of Jacob, the son of Isaac, the son of Abraham, the son of Terah, the son of Nahor,

Luke 3:38 – the son of Enos, the son of Seth, the son of Adam, the son of God.

Mary, Jesus' mother, is absent from Matthew's genealogy, since women were not customarily mentioned in Jewish genealogies. Joseph is mentioned as Heli's son, because he married Mary, Heli's daughter. Therefore, Jesus was legally a descendant of Abraham and David through Joseph, and biologically through Mary.

Luke 1:30-33 –
> 30 "And the angel [Gabriel] said to her [Mary], "Do not be afraid, Mary, for you have found favor with God. 31 And behold, you will conceive in your womb and bear a son, and you shall call his name Jesus. 32 He will be great and will be called the Son of the Most High. And the Lord God will give to him the throne of his father David, 33 and he will reign over the house of Jacob forever, and of his kingdom there will be no end."

The angel Gabriel told Mary that she would conceive and bring forth a Son that she would call Jesus. He would be God's Son, and God would give Him the throne of His father David, and He would rule Israel forever.

Application

When you lust, you reject following the King of righteousness, submitting instead to unrighteousness. Adam, Abraham, David, and the prophets longed for Jesus who would lead God's people faithfully into the eternal Promised Land. This King indwells you by His Holy Spirit. How then can you give yourself to lust or make excuses for it existing in your heart?

Lust leads you to the pit of despair and misery. Created for righteousness, ruined by sin, and now born again in Jesus, you must embody God's design for you: a life too holy for lust.

Lust distracts you from preparing for Christ's return. If the King returns today, you want Him to find you without spot or blemish (2 Pet 3:13-14), not entangled in lust. Though perfection escapes us in this life, it still must be our goal, because the King we serve is perfectly righteous, and we long to be like Him. He is transforming us into His likeness, and He will surely finish what He started in us in eternity.

Marching Orders: Thinking God's Thoughts After Him

Receive, believe, and live the truths you've read. Memorize and meditate on these truths today:

One Sentence to Shape Your Affections:

Jesus, the King of kings and Son of David, rules in righteousness over all creation on David's throne forever, while lust seeks to dethrone Christ in my heart.

One Poem to Shape Your Affections:

From David's line, as Nathan foretold,
His Son would shine, his throne to hold.
Jesus, in righteousness, would lead the way,
Freeing God's people from lust's dark sway.

Born of Mary, of Heli's sacred line,
Of Joseph's house, where lineages intertwine.
The angel said, Mary's womb would bring,
God's own Son, the everlasting King.

One Song to Shape Your Affections:

Add this song to your playlist, "See He Comes."

On YouTube,
By Sovereign Grace Music (Written by John Cennick, Charles Wesley, Rich
Gunderlock, and Zach Sprowls)

https://www.youtube.com/watch?v=BmphPqMdiy0

[Due to copyright laws, I cannot include the lyrics here, but they are included in
the above video.]

End with Prayer

Day 20

Jesus is Savior and Lord / Lust is Harm and Deception

Begin with Prayer

Scripture and Reflection

Matthew 1:21 – "She will bear a son, and you shall call his name Jesus, for he will save his people from their sins."

Luke 2:11 – For unto you is born this day in the city of David a Savior, who is Christ the Lord.

Acts 4:11-12 – 11 "This Jesus is the stone that was rejected by you, the builders, which has become the cornerstone. 12 And there is salvation in no one else, for there is no other name under heaven given among men by which we must be saved."

1 John 4:14 – And we have seen and testify that the Father has sent his Son to be the Savior of the world. 15 Whoever confesses that Jesus is the Son of God, God abides in him, and he in God.

Jesus Christ, God the Son Incarnate, came to save His people from their sins. As David's Son, He leads us in righteousness. And those who repent of sin and trust in Him, whether Jew or Gentile, will be eternally saved from God's wrath, this wicked world, their wicked hearts, and the evil one. No other Savior exists; He is the only Way of salvation.

Matthew 10:38-39 – [38] And whoever does not take his cross and follow me is not worthy of me. [39] Whoever finds his life will lose it, and whoever loses his life for my sake will find it.

Acts 2:29-36 –

> [29] "Brothers, I may say to you with confidence about the patriarch David that he both died and was buried, and his tomb is with us to this day. [30] Being therefore a prophet, and knowing that God had sworn with an oath to him that he would set one of his descendants on his throne, [31] he foresaw and spoke about the resurrection of the Christ, that he was not abandoned to Hades, nor did his flesh see corruption. [32] This Jesus God raised up, and of that we all are witnesses. [33] Being therefore exalted at the right hand of God, and having received from the Father the promise of the Holy Spirit, he has poured out this that you yourselves are seeing and hearing. [34] For David did not ascend into the heavens, but he himself says, "'The Lord said to my Lord, "Sit at my right hand, [35] until I make your enemies your footstool."'" [36] Let all the house of Israel therefore know for certain that God has made him both Lord and Christ, this Jesus whom you crucified."

Jesus is not only Savior but also Lord. He is the Christ, the Messiah, the fulfillment of all messianic prophecy. All who come to Him must trust in Him as both Savior and Lord, receiving not only His salvation, but also submitting to His morals as well. Since He is Lord, He demands our wholehearted devotion and service.

Application

When you lust, you submit to the devil, and the flesh that's in his likeness, as if they are your lord, rather than Christ. You embrace their immorality over Christ's

morality. Yet, the devil has only done you harm, never good; and Christ has only done you good, never harm. How then can you give yourself to your flesh?

When you lust, you affirm a temporary deception. Sin has never satisfied you, nor can it. Yet, you think this time will be different. You're deceiving yourself again, but you don't have to. The truth that Jesus is your Savior and Lord, and your faith in Him by His Holy Spirit, is enough for you to live righteously from your heart, because if Christ is Savior and Lord, then lust cannot satisfy you. Only He can.

How then should you live from your heart?

Marching Orders: Thinking God's Thoughts After Him

Receive, believe, and live the truths you've read. Memorize and meditate on these truths today:

One Sentence to Shape Your Affections:

Jesus is Savior and Lord, the only way to be saved from my sins and reconciled to God; while lust seeks to condemn me and alienate me from God.

One Poem to Shape Your Affections:

Jesus Christ, God's only Son,
Born to heal what lust had done.
Son of David, the promised King,
Hope to the world, His mercies bring.

Savior and Lord, no other Name,
Jesus, perfectly holy, forever the same.
He is the Way, the Truth, and the Life,
Saving from God's wrath, lust, and strife.
Lord and Christ, the Messiah true,

Fulfilling the word the prophets knew.
Bow to Him, both Lord and King,
Eternal Life, His love will bring.

One Song to Shape Your Affections:

Add this song to your playlist, "O Lord, My Rock and My Redeemer."

On YouTube,
By Sovereign Grace Music (Written by Nathan Stiff)

https://www.youtube.com/watch?v=yx5BB2J7R-8

[Due to copyright laws, I cannot include the lyrics here, but they are included in the above video.]

End with Prayer

Day 21

The Holy Spirit is God / Lust is Sinner-Made

Begin with Prayer

Scripture and Reflection

<u>Genesis 1:2</u> – The earth was without form and void, and darkness was over the face of the deep. And the Spirit of God was hovering over the face of the waters.

<u>Matthew 28:19</u> – Go therefore and make disciples of all nations, baptizing them in the name of the Father and of the Son and of the Holy Spirit,

<u>Psalm 104:30</u> – When you send forth your Spirit, they [creatures] are created, and you renew the face of the ground.

The Holy Spirit is truly God. He was in the beginning with the Father and the Son (Gen 1:1; John 1:1), creating out of nothing. To this day, God continues to create through His Son, by His Holy Spirit (Ps 104:30), and the church baptizes in the singular Name of the Father, Son, and Holy Spirit (Matt 28:19).

<u>Mark 3:28-29</u> – [28] "Truly, I say to you, all sins will be forgiven the children of man, and whatever blasphemies they utter, [29] but whoever blasphemes against the Holy Spirit never has forgiveness, but is guilty of an eternal sin"— [30] for they were saying, "He has an unclean spirit."

Mark 13:11 – And when they bring you to trial and deliver you over, do not be anxious beforehand what you are to say, but say whatever is given you in that hour, for it is not you who speak, but the Holy Spirit.

Luke 1:35 – And the angel answered her, "The Holy Spirit will come upon you, and the power of the Most High will overshadow you; therefore the child to be born will be called holy—the Son of God."

John 16:12-15 –

> 12 "I still have many things to say to you, but you cannot bear them now. 13 When the Spirit of truth comes, he will guide you into all the truth, for he will not speak on his own authority, but whatever he hears he will speak, and he will declare to you the things that are to come. 14 He will glorify me, for he will take what is mine and declare it to you. 15 All that the Father has is mine; therefore I said that he will take what is mine and declare it to you.

Acts 5:3-4 –

> 3 But Peter said, "Ananias, why has Satan filled your heart to lie to the Holy Spirit and to keep back for yourself part of the proceeds of the land? 4 While it remained unsold, did it not remain your own? And after it was sold, was it not at your disposal? Why is it that you have contrived this deed in your heart? You have not lied to man but to God."

Ephesians 4:30 – And do not grieve the Holy Spirit of God, by whom you were sealed for the day of redemption.

Romans 8:26-27 – 26 Likewise the Spirit helps us in our weakness. For we do not know what to pray for as we ought, but the Spirit himself intercedes for us with groanings too deep for words. 27 And he who searches hearts knows what is the mind of the Spirit, because the Spirit intercedes for the saints according to the will of God.

The Holy Spirit is truly God, one with the Father and Son, even as He is a distinct Divine Person:

1) He can be blasphemed (Mark 3:28-29).

2) He speaks (Mark 13:11).

3) He creates and sustains (Luke 1:35).

4) He guides Christ's disciples (John 16:12

5) He hears, declares, and glorifies Jesus (John 16:12-15).

6) He can be lied to and sinned against (Acts 5:3-4).

7) He can be grieved (Eph 4:30).

8) He intercedes for the saints (Rom 8:26-27).

9) He has a mind (Rom 8:27).

Far from being something less than truly God, like a force or power of God, or an angel or some other created being, the Holy Spirit is truly God. All that He does, He carries out distinctly among the Trinity, proceeding from the Father and the Son.

John 14:16-17 – [16] And I will ask the Father, and he will give you another Helper, to be with you forever, [17] even the Spirit of truth, whom the world cannot receive, because it neither sees him nor knows him. You know him, for he dwells with you and will be in you.

John 14:18 – "I will not leave you as orphans; I will come to you."

John 14:23 – Jesus answered him, "If anyone loves me, he will keep my word, and my Father will love him, and we will come to him and make our home with him."

John 15:26 – "But when the Helper comes, whom I will send to you from the Father, the Spirit of truth, who proceeds from the Father, he will bear witness about me."

John 16:7 – Nevertheless, I tell you the truth: it is to your advantage that I go away, for if I do not go away, the Helper will not come to you. But if I go, I will send him to you.

Jesus promised to send His Holy Spirit, who proceeds from His Father, to dwell within His disciples (John 14:16-17; 15:26; 16:7). Through the Spirit's presence in believers, the Father and Son also abide within us (John 14:18, 23).

These three Divine Persons, Father, Son, and Holy Spirit, are distinct even when they dwell within Christians. By the Holy Spirit, we receive the Father and Son as well, because these three Persons mutually indwell one Another (John 14:16-18, 23; 15:26; 16:7). To receive the Spirit is to receive the Trinity.

Application

When you lust, you follow what the devil has created in you, not what the Holy Spirit has created in you. The devil sinned first, then deceived Eve; she sinned, becoming like the devil, and Adam mindfully sinned, becoming like him too; and now, all of Adam's descendants are conceived in sin, and are sinners from conception. We're still created in God's image, but it has been marred by sin.

The devil was the first person to twist God's good creation. Lust, therefore, is from the devil, from Adam, not from God. When the Holy Spirit applies Christ's finished work to our hearts, through faith we are saved. The Holy Spirit remakes us and is remaking us in the image of Jesus Christ (Rom 8:29; 2 Cor 3:18). We must walk in the Spirit, in what He has done and is doing in us.

To live purely from our hearts is to image Christ, but to lust is to mirror the devil. We are indwelled by the Holy Spirit, Son, and Father; therefore, let us walk in Him, and not the evil one, not the flesh. When we trust in Christ, we're not just forgiven; we're empowered to live differently. Indwelled by the Holy Spirit, you are empowered to live His love, joy, peace, patience, kindness, goodness, gentleness, and self-control (Gal 5:16-26).

The question is if you will live what you have been empowered to do, from your heart, by the Holy Spirit. If you have been transformed by Him and are indwelled by the Trinity, how can you walk in the flesh? You must walk in the Spirit.

Today, commit to walk in Him. Pray for strength, set your heart on Christ, and take one step at a time toward a life that reflects Him. Tomorrow, do it again, and every day until you see Christ face to face in Heaven.

Marching Orders: Thinking God's Thoughts After Him

Receive, believe, and live the truths you've read. Memorize and meditate on these truths today:

One Sentence to Shape Your Affections:

The Holy Spirit is truly God, and by Him, the Father and Son live within all Christians, empowering me to turn from lust, turn to Christ, and kill the lust in my heart.

One Poem to Shape Your Affections:

Holy Spirit, with Father and Son, eternal,
My Seed of salvation, my Kernel.
He is neither angel, nor fleeting force,
But God Himself, creation's Source.

Distinct, Divine, a Person true,
He speaks, He guides, His will to do.
Grieved by lust, yet interceding,
He glorifies Christ, His people, leading.

Not a mere power, but God Most High,
On His mind and voice, the saints rely.
Sent by Jesus, from His Father's throne,
He dwells in me, I'm never alone.

Three yet One, in unity bound,
Father, Son, in Holy Spirit found.

Receiving the Spirit, Three Persons I gain,
God's love within me, forever to reign.

One Song to Shape Your Affections:

Add this song to your playlist, "Holy Spirit Living Breath of God."

On YouTube,
By Keith and Kristyn Getty (Written by Keith Getty and Stuart Townend)

https://www.youtube.com/watch?v=kDYjn-YdnD4

[Due to copyright laws, I cannot include the lyrics here, but they are included in the above video.]

End with Prayer

Day 22

The Holy Spirit is Life / Lust is a Murderer

Begin with Prayer

Scripture and Reflection

Ezekiel 36:26-27 – 26 And I will give you a new heart, and a new spirit I will put within you. And I will remove the heart of stone from your flesh and give you a heart of flesh. 27 And I will put my Spirit within you, and cause you to walk in my statutes and be careful to obey my rules.

John 3:5-6 – 5 Jesus answered, "Truly, truly, I say to you, unless one is born of water and the Spirit, he cannot enter the kingdom of God. 6 That which is born of the flesh is flesh, and that which is born of the Spirit is spirit."

Titus 3:5 – he saved us, not because of works done by us in righteousness, but according to his own mercy, by the washing of regeneration and renewal of the Holy Spirit.

In the Old Testament, Ezekiel prophesied about the new covenant, promising that God would transform His people by giving them a new heart and His Holy Spirit within them. This Divine Person would empower them to faithfully follow God's word and law. Jesus established the new covenant, teaching that all must be born again from above. Born from Adam's line, we are sinners, but through repentance and faith in Jesus Christ, the Holy Spirit regenerates and renews us through faith, uniting us to Christ.

Romans 8:9-11 –

> 9 You, however, are not in the flesh but in the Spirit, if in fact the Spirit of God dwells in you. Anyone who does not have the Spirit of Christ does not belong to him. 10 But if Christ is in you, although the body is dead because of sin, the Spirit is life because of righteousness. 11 If the Spirit of him who raised Jesus from the dead dwells in you, he who raised Christ Jesus from the dead will also give life to your mortal bodies through his Spirit who dwells in you.

1 Corinthians 6:11 – And such were some of you. But you were washed, you were sanctified, you were justified in the name of the Lord Jesus Christ and by the Spirit of our God.

The new covenant brings the transforming Gift who indwells all believers: the Holy Spirit. No longer defined by our lineage with Adam or our sinful flesh that is in his likeness, we are now defined by our union with Christ by the Spirit. Through Him, the Father and Son abide in us as well (John 14:16-18, 23; 15:26; 16:7). The Father, through the Son and by the Spirit, cleanses, sanctifies, and justifies us, declaring us righteous in Christ.

Galatians 5:22-25 –

> 22 But the fruit of the Spirit is love, joy, peace, patience, kindness, goodness, faithfulness, 23 gentleness, self-control; against such things there is no law. 24 And those who belong to Christ Jesus have crucified the flesh with its passions and desires. 25 If we live by the Spirit, let us also keep in step with the Spirit.

John 6:63 – It is the Spirit who gives life; the flesh is no help at all. The words that I have spoken to you are spirit and life.

The Holy Spirit dwells within us, not to leave us bound to the flesh, but to transform and empower us to live in step with Him. Through Christ, we have crucified the flesh, and the Spirit has brought us life. If we live by the Spirit, let us also walk with Him, by living out the fruit that He is producing in us: love, joy, peace, patience, kindness, goodness, faithfulness, gentleness, and self-control.

Application

When you lust, you live for what murdered you. The devil was a murderer from the beginning (John 8:44). He killed Adam and Eve by tempting them to sin, and they spiritually died when they submitted to him. From Adam's submission to the evil one, now we are conceived in sin, are spiritually dead, and death reigns in our lives until Christ by His Spirit comes into our lives and changes us, causing us to be born again in Him (Rom 8:9-11). The Holy Spirit is life and lust is death.

When you lust, you turn back to what God has saved you from. You left sin behind to follow Christ. You left your flesh's desires behind when you trusted in Christ for salvation. To give in to it now, is to live contrary to who you are in Jesus Christ. You've been born again, born from above, to live the ethics from above, and to forsake the ways from below, the ways of the world.

Finally, when you lust, you live like the flesh gives you life. Yet the flesh can only produce sin and death (James 1:13-15); it always lies when it whispers of joy and happiness. To trust that deception is to doubt Christ, who said, "It is the Spirit who gives life; the flesh is no help at all" (John 6:63). When Jesus tells us to repent, He's telling us to leave lust and its empty promises behind, and to embrace Him, who is righteousness and true life.

Today, will you embrace true life in Christ, or will you embrace death in lust?

Marching Orders: Thinking God's Thoughts After Him

Receive, believe, and live the truths you've read. Memorize and meditate on these truths today:

141

One Sentence to Shape Your Affections:

The Holy Spirit brings eternal life by regenerating me, sanctifying me, and empowering me to live out the fruit He is producing in my heart; while lust cuts me, injures me, and hinders my relationship with God.

One Poem to Shape Your Affections:

In Ezekiel, a new covenant, God's promise foretold,
A new heart, a new Spirit, on the same old road.
My heart from stone to flesh, God's Spirit within,
Empowers me to walk in Him, not imputing sin.

Born again, from above, as Jesus decreed,
By Spirit and water, from lust I am freed.
No longer in Adam, but united to Christ's name,
The Spirit regenerates, ignites me in holy flame.

He indwells me, with the Father and Son,
In Christ we're united, our hearts becoming one.
Washed, justified, and sanctified, by His hand,
Declared righteous in Him, on His promise I stand.

No longer in the flesh, but alive in the Spirit,
Crucified with Christ, His life I inherit.
Love, joy, and peace, His fruit I now bear,
Walking with the Spirit till His glory, I share.

One Song to Shape Your Affections:

Add this song to your playlist, "All I Have is Christ."

On YouTube,
By Jordan Kauflin

142

https://www.youtube.com/watch?v=jg_gl3IpEFw

[Due to copyright laws, I cannot include the lyrics here, but they are included in the above video.]

End with Prayer

Day 23

Jesus Baptizes us with the Holy Spirit / Lust Immerses us in Death

Begin with Prayer

Scripture and Reflection

Matthew 3:11-12 –

> [John the Baptist preached,] 11 "I baptize you with water for repentance, but he who is coming after me is mightier than I, whose sandals I am not worthy to carry. He will baptize you with the Holy Spirit and fire. 12 His winnowing fork is in his hand, and he will clear his threshing floor and gather his wheat into the barn, but the chaff he will burn with unquenchable fire."

John 14:15-17 – 15 "If you love me, you will keep my commandments. 16 And I will ask the Father, and he will give you another Helper, to be with you forever, 17 even the Spirit of truth, whom the world cannot receive, because it neither sees him nor knows him. You know him, for he dwells with you and will be in you."

John the Baptist came to prepare the way for YHWH the Son. He came preaching repentance and requiring that his hearers show evidence of repentance before he baptized them (Matt 3:8; Luke 3:8). He also prophesied of Jesus baptizing His disciples with the Holy Spirit. Jesus later told His disciples that He would leave them but would send the Holy Spirit to help them. The Spirit was already *with* them, but when Jesus sent Him, He would be *in* them.

Acts 1:5 – [Jesus said to His disciples before He ascended to heaven,] "for John baptized with water, but you will be baptized with the Holy Spirit not many days from now."

Acts 2:1-4 –

When the day of Pentecost arrived, they were all together in one place. ² And suddenly there came from heaven a sound like a mighty rushing wind, and it filled the entire house where they were sitting. ³ And divided tongues as of fire appeared to them and rested on each one of them. ⁴ And they were all filled with the Holy Spirit and began to speak in other tongues as the Spirit gave them utterance.

Acts 2:14-21 –

[After hearing people accuse the disciples of being drunk because they were speaking in foreign languages they had not learned,] ¹⁴ But Peter, standing with the eleven, lifted up his voice and addressed them: "Men of Judea and all who dwell in Jerusalem, let this be known to you, and give ear to my words. ¹⁵ For these people are not drunk, as you suppose, since it is only the third hour of the day. ¹⁶ But this is what was uttered through the prophet Joel [Joel 2:28-32]: ¹⁷ 'And in the last days it shall be, God declares, that I will pour out my Spirit on all flesh, and your sons and your daughters shall prophesy, and your young men shall see visions, and your old men shall dream dreams; ¹⁸ even on my male servants and female servants in those days I will pour out my Spirit, and they shall prophesy. ¹⁹ And I will show wonders in the heavens above and signs on the earth below, blood, and fire, and vapor of smoke; ²⁰ the sun shall be turned to darkness and the moon to blood, before the day of the Lord comes, the great and magnificent day. ²¹ And it shall come to pass that everyone who calls upon the name of the Lord shall be saved.'"

In the upper room, the disciples were filled with the Holy Spirit. A multitude of Jews from every nation gathered, hearing them proclaim God's mighty works in their own languages. Some mocked, claiming they were drunk, but Peter scoffed that it was only 9 in the morning. Instead, he preached that they were filled with the Holy Spirit, as the prophet Joel foretold (Joel 2:28-32) and as Jesus promised a few days earlier (Acts 1:5).

<u>Romans 8:9-11</u> –

> [9] You, however, are not in the flesh but in the Spirit, if in fact the Spirit of God dwells in you. Anyone who does not have the Spirit of Christ does not belong to him. [10] But if Christ is in you, although the body is dead because of sin, the Spirit is life because of righteousness. [11] If the Spirit of him who raised Jesus from the dead dwells in you, he who raised Christ Jesus from the dead will also give life to your mortal bodies through his Spirit who dwells in you.

The apostle Paul taught that all Christians are in the Spirit, and no longer in the flesh. Through faith in Christ, the Holy Spirit dwells within every believer. Although we are dead because of sin, the Holy Spirit has given us life, empowering us to walk with Him and live for Jesus.

Application

When you lust, you reject what John the Baptist prepared the way for. Not only did He prepare the way for Christ, he prepared the way for Christ's morals or ethics, Christ's fulfilment of God's law. You trust in Christ; therefore, you must live His ethics, because Christ sent His Holy Spirit to enable you to live for Him.

When you lust, you devalue what the prophet Joel longed for, the indwelling of the Holy Spirit in God's people. Through faith in Christ, God dwells in you by His Spirit, a Gift not given to unbelievers. How then can you take this affection for the indwelling of the Holy Spirit, what the prophets longed for, and give it to what the devil longs for, God's people immersed in lust?

Finally, when you lust, you live for the flesh, which is dead. To play with lust is to play with a corpse, when you have God, who is Life, living inside you.

Today, will you live for who John the Baptist prepared the way for, for what the prophet Joel longed for, for life, not death? Then, you must repent of lust.

Marching Orders: Thinking God's Thoughts After Him

Receive, believe, and live the truths you've read. Memorize and meditate on these truths today:

One Sentence to Shape Your Affections:

John prepared the way for Christ to baptize His disciples with the Holy Spirit, as the prophet Joel foretold, who all Christians are immersed in through faith in Christ, while lust seeks to immerse me in sin and death.

One Poem to Shape Your Affections:

John the Baptist cleared the path,
For YHWH's Son, he preached with wrath.
"Repent, bear fruit!" his cry rang true,
Before he'd baptize, a heart must be new.

Christ baptizes with His Spirit to flame,
To raise the spiritually dead, to guide, to claim.
Jesus promised, though He'd depart,
The Spirit's power would fill each believing heart.

In the upper room, the disciples prayed,
The Spirit came, their fears, He slayed.
Languages aflame, a rushing wind,
God's mighty work, their voices to send.

From every nation, Jews drew near,
God's word, in their languages, to hear.
Some scoffed, "They're drunk!" but Peter did cry,

"It's too early for new wine, hear Joel prophesy."
Paul declared, in Christ we rise,
The Spirit dwells where faith abides.
Though once dead in lust and flesh, Christ I gain,
By the Father's hand, I walk in the Spirit's reign.

One Song to Shape Your Affections:

Add this song to your playlist, "He Leadeth Me."

On YouTube,
By Sovereign Grace Music (Written by Joseph Gilmore and William Bradbury)

https://www.youtube.com/watch?v=rpYM6Et_hVY

1. He leadeth me; O blessed thought!
O words with heav'nly comfort fraught!
Whate'er I do, where'er I be,
Still 'tis God's hand that leadeth me.

Refrain: He leadeth me, He leadeth me;
By His own hand He leadeth me;
His faithful follower I would be,
For by His hand He leadeth me.

2. Sometimes 'mid scenes of deepest gloom,
Sometimes where Eden's flowers bloom,
By waters still, o'er troubled sea,
Still 'tis His hand that leadeth me.

3. Lord, I would clasp Thy hand in mine,
Nor ever murmur, nor repine,
Content, whatever lot I see, since
'Tis Thy hand that leadeth me.

4. And when my task on earth is done,
When, by Thy grace, the victory's won,
E'en death's cold wave I will not flee,
Since God through Jordan leadeth me.[21]

End with Prayer

[21] "He Leadeth Me," Hymnary, Accessed September 13, 2025,
https://hymnary.org/text/he_leadeth_me_o_blessed_thought.

Day 24

Think on God, Develop Patterns of Righteousness / Think on Lust, Develop Patterns of Evil

Begin with Prayer

Scripture and Reflection

Psalm 115:1-8 –

> Not to us, O Lord, not to us, but to your name give glory, for the sake of your steadfast love and your faithfulness! ² Why should the nations say, "Where is their God?" ³ Our God is in the heavens; he does all that he pleases. ⁴ Their idols are silver and gold, the work of human hands. ⁵ They have mouths, but do not speak; eyes, but do not see. ⁶ They have ears, but do not hear; noses, but do not smell. ⁷ They have hands, but do not feel; feet, but do not walk; and they do not make a sound in their throat. ⁸ Those who make them become like them; so do all who trust in them.

The Psalmist told us that we become like whatever we think on (Ps 115:1-8). In other words, we become like what we worship. Those who love idols, whether false gods or various lusts, grow to resemble their worthlessness. In contrast, those who worship YHWH are transformed into His likeness, reflecting His goodness and truth. This is why the Ten Commandments, and the two greatest commandments begin with loving God above all (Ex 20; Matt 22:37-39). He must be at the top of our lives or we are aimed at evil.

Philippians 4:8-13 –

> 8 Finally, brothers, whatever is true, whatever is honorable, whatever is just, whatever is pure, whatever is lovely, whatever is commendable, if there is any excellence, if there is anything worthy of praise, think about these things. 9 What you have learned and received and heard and seen in me—practice these things, and the God of peace will be with you. 10 I rejoiced in the Lord greatly that now at length you have revived your concern for me. You were indeed concerned for me, but you had no opportunity. 11 Not that I am speaking of being in need, for I have learned, in whatever situation I am, to be content. 12 I know how to be brought low, and I know how to abound. In any and every circumstance, I have learned the secret of facing plenty and hunger, abundance and need. 13 I can do all things through him who strengthens me.

James 1:13-15 –

> "13 Let no one say when he is tempted, "I am being tempted by God," for God cannot be tempted with evil, and he himself tempts no one. 14 But each person is tempted when he is lured and enticed by his own desire. 15 Then desire when it has conceived gives birth to sin, and sin when it is fully grown brings forth death.

The apostle Paul, writing from prison, urged the church at Philippi to think on all that is good, true, and beautiful, so that they would have peace. Why? Because Paul understood how to be brought low and how to abound. He could do all things through Christ who strengthened him (Phil 4:11-13), for to him, to live was Christ and to die was gain (Phil 1:21). When you're content with Christ, no circumstance, whether good or ill, can take Him or your contentment in Him away from you.

James spoke similarly but from the opposite angle. Just as thinking on the good, true, and beautiful, brings you peace, thinking on sin brings you death (James 1:14-15). Sin begins in our hearts as tempting impulses against God, as the lusts of the flesh. Once our lusts lure and entice us, sin is mindfully conceived, and it grows into death. That's the life cycle of sin: lust, mindful sin, then death.

If you think on miserable, wicked, and ungodly things, then you become miserable, wicked, and ungodly. But if you think on good, true, and beautiful things, you become more like God (if you're a Christian).

All that is good, true, and beautiful comes from God, directly or indirectly. In contrast, all that is miserable, wicked, and ungodly, comes from Satan, directly or indirectly. God permits the devil and his sin for His greater glory, but the evil one will be judged eternally. Only God and His goodness endures forever.

Romans 1:18-32 –

[18] For the wrath of God is revealed from heaven against all ungodliness and unrighteousness of men, who by their unrighteousness suppress the truth. [19] For what can be known about God is plain to them, because God has shown it to them. [20] For his invisible attributes, namely, his eternal power and divine nature, have been clearly perceived, ever since the creation of the world, in the things that have been made. So they are without excuse. [21] For although they knew God, they did not honor him as God or give thanks to him, but they became futile in their thinking, and their foolish hearts were darkened. [22] Claiming to be wise, they became fools, [23] and exchanged the glory of the immortal God for images resembling mortal man and birds and animals and creeping things. [24] Therefore God gave them up in the lusts of their hearts to impurity, to the dishonoring of their bodies among themselves, [25] because they exchanged the truth about God for a lie and worshiped and served the creature rather than the Creator, who is blessed forever! Amen. [26] For this reason God gave them up to dishonorable passions. For their women exchanged natural relations for those that are contrary to nature; [27] and the men likewise gave up natural relations with women and were consumed with passion for one another, men committing shameless acts with men and receiving in themselves the due penalty for their error. [28] And since they did not see fit to acknowledge God, God gave them up to a debased mind to do what ought not to be done. [29] They were filled with all manner of unrighteousness, evil, covetousness, malice. They are full of envy, murder, strife, deceit, maliciousness. They are gossips, [30] slanderers,

haters of God, insolent, haughty, boastful, inventors of evil, disobedient to parents, [31] foolish, faithless, heartless, ruthless. [32] Though they know God's righteous decree that those who practice such things deserve to die, they not only do them but give approval to those who practice them.

Romans 6:19 – I am speaking in human terms, because of your natural limitations. For just as you once presented your members as slaves to impurity and to lawlessness leading to more lawlessness, so now present your members as slaves to righteousness leading to sanctification.

Paul warns that worshipping created things rather than the Creator leads to a darkened mind, upside-down sexuality, and patterns of all kinds of sin (Rom 1:21-28). In contrast, worshipping God does the opposite: it leads to a sound mind, upright sexuality, and patterns of all kinds of righteousness (Rom 6:19).

Application

When you lust, it pulls you to become a little more lustful and a little less obedient to God. You mirror the evil one a little more and Christ a little less. Yet, as a believer, you are forever justified in Christ by grace through faith (Rom 5:1). Lust contradicts this truth, pulling you toward patterns of sin instead of the patterns of righteousness you're called to embody (Rom 6:1-2).

When you lust, you believe the lustful lies of your flesh that you're thinking on good, truth, and beauty, but it's a mirage; you're really thinking on misery, wickedness, and ungodliness. And these three evils harm your relationships with others as well, because thinking on evil can only foster selfishness in your heart rather than love.

When you lust, you place your sinful appetites above God, hungering for sin instead of His righteousness (Matt 5:6). And you give your time and devotion to evil: time that could be spent seeking God's glory. Through God's Holy Spirit living within you, you can turn from lust and fix your mind on what is good, true, and beautiful.

Today, will you turn from lust and choose to pursue and think on God's beauty and all that pleases Him? You can, but will you?

Marching Orders: Thinking God's Thoughts After Him

Receive, believe, and live the truths you've read. Memorize and meditate on these truths today:

One Sentence to Shape Your Affections:

My impulses, thoughts, actions, and patterns shape me for good or for ill: dwelling on God and His righteousness, transforms me into His image, but fixating on lust makes me reflect Satan.

One Poem to Shape Your Affections:

I become like what I think on,
Idols I chase, or God's own Son.
From prison, Paul tells me to dwell,
On good, truth, beauty, not what leads to hell.

In Christ, Paul thrived in prosperity or pain,
For to him, to live was Christ, and death was gain.
James warns: If lust in my heart takes root,
It spawns mindful sin, death's bitter fruit.

All that's good flows from God's perfect throne,
But evil has a source and path all its own.
Choose the soil where righteousness will bloom,
Or cling to lust and reap sin's barren tomb.

One Song to Shape Your Affections:

Add this song to your playlist, "Hast Thou Heard Him, Seen Him, Known Him?"

On YouTube,
By Indelible Grace Music (Written by Ora Rowan)

https://www.youtube.com/watch?v=bIrURZ389oo

1. Hast thou heard Him, seen Him, known Him?
Is not thine a captured heart?
Chief among ten thousand own Him,
Joyful choose the better part.

Chorus: Captivated by His beauty, Worthy tribute haste to bring.
Let His peerless worth constrain thee, Crown Him now unrivaled King.

2. What can strip the seeming beauty,
From the idols of the earth?
Not a sense of right or duty,
But the sight of peerless worth.

3. 'Tis that look that melted Peter,
'Tis that face that Stephen saw,
'Tis that heart that wept with Mary,
Can alone from idols draw.[22]

End with Prayer

---

[22] "Hast Thou Heard Him, Seen Him, Known Him?" Indelible Grace Hymn Book, Accessed September 13, 2025, https://ighymns.herokuapp.com/hymns/hast-thou-heard-him-seen-him-known-him.

Day 25

God Says We're Marvelously Made / Lust Destroys us From Within

Begin with Prayer

Scripture and Reflection

Psalm 139:13-16 –

> ¹³ For you formed my inward parts; you knitted me together in my mother's womb. ¹⁴ I praise you, for I am fearfully and wonderfully made. Wonderful are your works; my soul knows it very well. ¹⁵ My frame was not hidden from you, when I was being made in secret, intricately woven in the depths of the earth. ¹⁶ Your eyes saw my unformed substance; in your book were written, every one of them, the days that were formed for me, when as yet there was none of them.

In our mothers' wombs, God made each of us, crafting us marvelously so that we would reflect Him. Even as embryos, He knew and designed us, and charted our days before we were even conceived.

1 Corinthians 6:13-20 –

> The body is not meant for sexual immorality, but for the Lord, and the Lord for the body. ¹⁴ And God raised the Lord and will also raise us up by his power. ¹⁵ Do you not know that your bodies are members of Christ? Shall I

then take the members of Christ and make them members of a prostitute? Never! 16 Or do you not know that he who is joined to a prostitute becomes one body with her? For, as it is written, "The two will become one flesh." 17 But he who is joined to the Lord becomes one spirit with him. 18 Flee from sexual immorality. Every other sin a person commits is outside the body, but the sexually immoral person sins against his own body. 19 Or do you not know that your body is a temple of the Holy Spirit within you, whom you have from God? You are not your own, 20 for you were bought with a price. So glorify God in your body.

God designed our bodies not for sexual immorality or lust, but for the Lord. The same is true for everyone. And Christians, by the Holy Spirit through faith in Christ, our bodies are no longer our own but are one with Him, for we were bought with a great price. We are the temple of God. We are so united to Christ that to participate in sexual immorality, we must take what is united to Christ, ourselves, and unite to whatever object we desire. This is true even when we lust in our hearts, though outward sexual immorality is a more heinous sin.

Paul urges us to flee sexual immorality because it is different from other sins in that we sin against our own bodies (1 Cor 6:18). There is an intimacy and closeness associated with sexual sin that is not present in sins "outside the body." Sexual sin destroys the body from within as lust enslaves us. This sin objectifies both the person targeted and the one consumed by evil desire, diminishing the value and humanity of both.[23]

Genesis 1:26-27 –

26 Then God said, "Let us make man in our image, after our likeness. And let them have dominion over the fish of the sea and over the birds of the heavens and over the livestock and over all the earth and over every creeping thing that creeps on the earth." 27 So God created man in his own image, in the image of God he created him; male and female he created them.

---

[23] Herman Bavinck, *Reformed Ethics, Volume 1: Created, Fallen, and Converted Humanity*, ed. John Bolt, trans. Nelson D. Kloosterman (Grand Rapids: Baker Academic, 2019), 248.

<u>Genesis 3:1-6</u> –

Now the serpent was more crafty than any other beast of the field that the Lord God had made. He said to the woman, "Did God actually say, 'You shall not eat of any tree in the garden'?" ² And the woman said to the serpent, "We may eat of the fruit of the trees in the garden, ³ but God said, 'You shall not eat of the fruit of the tree that is in the midst of the garden, neither shall you touch it, lest you die.'" ⁴ But the serpent said to the woman, "You will not surely die. ⁵ For God knows that when you eat of it your eyes will be opened, and you will be like God, knowing good and evil." ⁶ So when the woman saw that the tree was good for food, and that it was a delight to the eyes, and that the tree was to be desired to make one wise, she took of its fruit and ate, and she also gave some to her husband who was with her, and he ate.

Because lust is the objectification of an image-bearer, it is not the enjoyment of beauty. Rather, you're *sinfully* enjoying the object's beauty, which means you're enjoying a sinful twisting of the person's beauty, not his or her beauty as God intended, which is for His glory and potentially for a spouse to enjoy.

It is not beauty that compels you but sin. Just as Eve was not tempted by the forbidden tree until she believed the serpent instead of God (Gen 3:1-6), you too are not tempted by another person's beauty until you believe your flesh or the devil instead of God. It is not God's creating excellence that tempts you but your sinful heart, just as it was not the forbidden tree that tempted Eve but the devil.

Moreover, instead of seeing the person you're lusting after as created in God's image, you see him or her as created to reflect a false god. By using the person contrary to God's design, you de-person/de-image him or her to reflect evil. You thus necessarily affirm the lie that some humans were *not* created in God's image.

Finally, you go against God's will. God willed to make mankind in His image, male and female. How we are permitted to view one another must be in lock step with God's design. We must think God's thoughts after Him. He does not permit us to lust after one another. Every lustful inclination, thought, desire, or action is against the will of God.

Application

When you lust, you live like God designed your body for sexual immorality and not for the Lord. Eve was created from Adam's body to be joined again with his body when the two became one flesh in marriage (Gen 2:18-25). They were not created to sexually desire multiple people, and neither were you. Lust distorts God's design, devaluing both the person you desire and yourself as image-bearers. It reduces others to objects and erodes your own humanity, pulling you away from God's intent.

When you lust, you call, "beautiful," what God calls, "ugly." Your body was not meant for sexual immorality but to please the Lord; therefore, each lustful impulse, desire, thought, or action turns God's design upside down, calling it "good," thinking that it will satisfy you. But, by definition, as God's image-bearer, and through faith, His child, you can never find satisfaction anywhere but in God.

Today, will you value others and yourself as God's image-bearers? Will you agree with God that only His design for your body is beautiful, and everything contrary to His design is ugly? Will you only use your body and the bodies of others for the Lord, to fulfill His beautiful design?

Marching Orders: Thinking God's Thoughts After Him

Receive, believe, and live the truths you've read. Memorize and meditate on these truths today:

One Sentence to Shape Your Affections:

My body was created for God's glory, not sexual immorality, so any lustful impulse, desire, thought, or action devalues both others and me as His image-bearers.

One Poem to Shape Your Affections:

By God, in the womb, I'm fearfully made,

His image displayed, His plans arrayed.
Before my breath, He wove my embryo,
Designed my days, my heart, my soul.

Not for lust was my body formed,
But for the Lord, by love transformed.
United to Christ, I'm not my own,
Yet my lust lures me, and seeds are sown.

Lust twists God's beauty, blinds my eye,
Sees not His glory but embraces a lie.
It hides His image, cloaks its light,
And aims at a false god of blackest night.

God's will be clear: I must reflect His light,
And see males and females with holy sight.
Lust defies His will, distorts His plan,
And robs my soul of what it is to be man.

One Song to Shape Your Affections:

Add this song to your playlist, "Guide Me O Thou Great Jehovah."

On YouTube,
By Indelible Grace Music (Written by William Williams and Jeremy Casella)

https://www.youtube.com/watch?v=SCqSlYY8mwc

1. Guide me, O Thou great Jehovah,
Pilgrim through this barren land.
I am weak, but Thou art mighty;
Hold me with Thy powerful hand.
Bread of heaven,
Feed me now and evermore;

Bread of heaven,
Feed me now and evermore.

2. Open now the crystal fountain,
Whence the healing waters flow;
Let the fire and cloudy pillar
Lead me all my journey through.
Strong Deliverer,
Be Thou still my Strength and Shield.
Strong Deliverer,
Be Thou still my Strength and Shield.

3. When I tread the verge of Jordan,
Bid my anxious fears subside;
Death of death, and hell's destruction,
Land me safe on Canaan's side.
Songs of praises, I will ever give to Thee;
Songs of praises, I will ever give to Thee.[24]

End with Prayer

---

[24] "Guide Me," Hymnary, Accessed September 13, 2025,
https://hymnary.org/text/guide_me_o_thou_great_jehovah.

Day 26

The Lord Forgives and Gives Eternal Life / Lust Brings Death and Hell

Begin with Prayer

Scripture and Reflection

Proverbs 2:16-19 – [16] So you will be delivered from the forbidden woman, from the adulteress with her smooth words, [17] who forsakes the companion of her youth and forgets the covenant of her God; [18] for her house sinks down to death, and her paths to the departed; [19] none who go to her come back, nor do they regain the paths of life.

Proverbs 5:1-6 –

My son, be attentive to my wisdom; incline your ear to my understanding, [2] that you may keep discretion, and your lips may guard knowledge. [3] For the lips of a forbidden woman drip honey, and her speech is smoother than oil, [4] but in the end she is bitter as wormwood, sharp as a two-edged sword. [5] Her feet go down to death; her steps follow the path to Sheol; [6] she does not ponder the path of life; her ways wander, and she does not know it.

Proverbs 6:23-24 – [23] For the commandment is a lamp and the teaching a light, and the reproofs of discipline are the way of life, [24] to preserve you from the evil woman, from the smooth tongue of the adulteress.

<u>Proverbs 7:24-25</u> – ²⁴ And now, O sons, listen to me, and be attentive to the words of my mouth. ²⁵ Let not your heart turn aside to her ways; do not stray into her paths, ²⁶ for many a victim has she laid low, and all her slain are a mighty throng. ²⁷ Her house is the way to Sheol, going down to the chambers of death.

Men and women, including pornographers, who tempt others into sexual immorality or adultery use smooth, seductive words to lure their victims toward destruction, even eternal hell. They stand in open graves, dressed in immodest clothes, as they seek to entice others to join them. Solomon compares the adulterous woman to a merciless serial killer, for "none who go to her come back, nor do they regain the paths of life (Prov 2:19)" and "many a victim has she laid low, and all her slain are a mighty throng" (Prov 7:26). She's the stalking slasher in a horror movie, and you're the foolish victim that hides in stupid places instead of fighting or fleeing. If you give in, sin will consume you, binding you to misery and death, and possibly hell itself.

<u>Matthew 18:7-9</u> –

> ⁷ "Woe to the world for temptations to sin! For it is necessary that temptations come, but woe to the one by whom the temptation comes! ⁸ And if your hand or your foot causes you to sin, cut it off and throw it away. It is better for you to enter life crippled or lame than with two hands or two feet to be thrown into the eternal fire. ⁹ And if your eye causes you to sin, tear it out and throw it away. It is better for you to enter life with one eye than with two eyes to be thrown into the hell of fire."

It's not only the adulterous man, woman, or pornography that tempts us. Jesus linked the command against tempting others directly to the peril of tempting oneself. Your greatest problem isn't other people; it's your own heart that finds evil enticing. We tempt ourselves, and Jesus demands a radical response: not to cut off the tempter's hand but our own, and not to cut out the tempter's eye but our own.

We must respond to our sinful impulses or lusts, with radical repentance. Christ's hyperbolic commands against inward temptation are drastic, but no more radical than His warning to the man that tempts His disciples: "It would be better for him to have a great millstone fastened around his neck and to be drowned in the depth of the sea" (Matt 18:6). Whether temptation comes from within or from without, Christ's followers must reject it decisively, for it descends to death and hell, and will drag us there too if it can.

Application

When you lust, it's like embracing a serial-killer and expecting to walk away unharmed. You'd laugh at a movie plot that naïve or yell at the screen in disbelief, but you're even more foolish. Remember why you turned to Christ in the first place: the empty promises of the lust-driven world left you hollow and miserable. You left it behind for good reason. Do not return now and embrace death and hell, when you have tasted eternal life in Christ.

When you lust, instead of congratulating yourself for "just looking" or surviving another tempting day, recognize lust for the thief it is, one that steals your joy, peace, and closeness to God. Jesus Himself warned us to take radical action: "if your eye causes you to sin, tear it out and throw it away. It is better for you to enter life with one eye than with two eyes to be thrown into the hell of fire" (Matt 18:9). If TV shows, movies, or the Internet tempt you or cause you to sin, cut them out; cancel subscriptions, install filters, or cancel them altogether. If a co-worker is enticing you, no longer talk with him or her, or ask for a transfer, or quit and find a new job. If your friends tempt you with lustful living, cut off contact with them and find some godly friends (1 Cor 15:33).

Whatever you do, don't embrace death and hell. If you do, you may never fully recover from the damage and consequences in this life. The Lord forgives and saves eternally but there are consequences for sin in this life that may last until we go to be with Him.

Marching Orders: Thinking God's Thoughts After Him

Receive, believe, and live the truths you've read. Memorize and meditate on these truths today:

One Sentence to Shape Your Affections:

Tempters and pornography are serial killers that stand in death and hell and will drag me there if possible.

One Poem to Shape Your Affections:

Smooth words weave a deadly spell,
Enticing hearts to death and hell.
In graves they stand, immodest, bold,
Luring souls to chains untold.

Serial killers stalking in the night,
Adulterers slay with fake delight.
None return from her embrace,
Lost forever away from Christ's face.

Yet deeper still, the tempter lives within,
My heart seduces me with lust and sin.
Christ's call is clear, severe, and true:
"Cut off your hand that tempts you."

Let no eye wander, nor touch betray,
Lest death and hell claim me as prey.
With millstone weight, the tempter is doomed,
If I repent, reject, I'll see them entombed.

One Song Often to Shape Your Affections:

Add this song to your playlist, "Jesus, I My Cross Have Taken."

On YouTube,

By Indelible Grace Music (Written by Henry Lyte)

https://www.youtube.com/watch?v=MMt-fCDpQ78

1. Jesus, I my cross have taken,
All to leave and follow Thee.
Destitute, despised, forsaken,
Thou from hence my all shall be.
Perish every fond ambition,
All I've sought or hoped or known.
Yet how rich is my condition!
God and heaven are still my own.

2. Let the world despise and leave me,
They have left my Savior, too.
Human hearts and looks deceive me;
Thou art not, like them, untrue.
O while Thou dost smile upon me,
God of wisdom, love, and might,
Foes may hate and friends disown me,
Show Thy face and all is bright.

3. Man may trouble and distress me,
Twill but drive me to Thy breast.
Life with trials hard may press me;
Heaven will bring me sweeter rest.
Oh, tis not in grief to harm me
While Thy love is left to me;
Oh, twere not in joy to charm me,
Were that joy unmixed with Thee.

4. Go, then, earthly fame and treasure,
Come disaster, scorn and pain
In Thy service, pain is pleasure,
With Thy favor, loss is gain
I have called Thee Abba Father,
I have stayed my heart on Thee
Storms may howl, and clouds may gather;
All must work for good to me.

5. Soul, then know thy full salvation
Rise o'er sin and fear and care
Joy to find in every station,
Something still to do or bear.
Think what Spirit dwells within thee,
Think what Father's smiles are thine,
Think that Jesus died to win thee,
Child of heaven, canst thou repine.

6. Haste thee on from grace to glory,
Armed by faith, and winged by prayer.
Heaven's eternal days before thee,
God's own hand shall guide us there.
Soon shall close thy earthly mission,
Soon shall pass thy pilgrim days,
Hope shall change to glad fruition,
Faith to sight, and prayer to praise.[25]

End with Prayer

---

[25] "Jesus, I My Cross Have Taken," Hymnary, Accessed September 13, 2025, https://hymnary.org/text/jesus_i_my_cross_have_taken_all_to_le.

Day 27

God Created us for Marriage / Lust Says we Were Created for Sex

Begin with Prayer

Scripture and Reflection

Genesis 2:18-25 –

18 Then the Lord God said, "It is not good for the man to be alone; I will make him a helper suitable for him." 19 And out of the ground the Lord God formed every animal of the field and every bird of the sky, and brought them to the man to see what he would call them; and whatever the man called a living creature, that was its name. 20 The man gave names to all the livestock, and to the birds of the sky, and to every animal of the field, but for Adam there was not found a helper suitable for him. 21 So the Lord God caused a deep sleep to fall upon the man, and he slept; then He took one of his ribs and closed up the flesh at that place. 22 And the Lord God fashioned into a woman the rib which He had taken from the man, and brought her to the man. 23 Then the man said, "At last this is bone of my bones, And flesh of my flesh; She shall be called 'woman,' Because she was taken out of man." 24 For this reason a man shall leave his father and his mother, and be joined to his wife; and they shall become one flesh. 25 And the man and his wife were both naked, but they were not ashamed.

In the beginning, Adam named all the animals, exercising the dominion God had given him, but there was no complementary human for him. So, God put him in a deep sleep, took one of his ribs and formed Eve. Adam then was missing a piece of his own body. And that rib, now Eve, was missing being part of him as well. God brought the two back together in marriage to become husband and wife, to become one flesh: "For this reason a man shall leave his father and his mother, and be joined to his wife; and they shall become one flesh" (Gen 2:24).

Therefore, all males and females are missing a piece of their bodies, until they pursue an opposite-sex Christian to marry, according to Scripture. You could say that marriage is in the DNA of every human being. Marriage is the rule and singleness is the exception. Paul says, due to the distress in Corinth at the time, singleness was preferrable, for devotion to the Lord, but each had his gift from the Lord (1 Cor 7:7, 26). Thus, marriage requires being born male or female and being single requires an extra gift of singleness from the Lord, not found in creation. Unbelievers do not possess this gift; though they possess the gift of marriage because they were created male or female.

Ephesians 5:25-33 –

25 Husbands, love your wives, as Christ loved the church and gave himself up for her, 26 that he might sanctify her, having cleansed her by the washing of water with the word, 27 so that he might present the church to himself in splendor, without spot or wrinkle or any such thing, that she might be holy and without blemish. 28 In the same way husbands should love their wives as their own bodies. He who loves his wife loves himself. 29 For no one ever hated his own flesh, but nourishes and cherishes it, just as Christ does the church, 30 because we are members of his body. 31 "Therefore a man shall leave his father and mother and hold fast to his wife, and the two shall become one flesh." 32 This mystery is profound, and I am saying that it refers to Christ and the church. 33 However, let each one of you love his wife as himself, and let the wife see that she respects her husband.

John 3:29-30 – [John the Baptist said,] "²⁹ The one who has the bride is the bridegroom. The friend of the bridegroom, who stands and hears him, rejoices greatly at the bridegroom's voice. Therefore this joy of mine is now complete. ³⁰ He must increase, but I must decrease."

Revelation 19:6-9 –

> ⁶ Then I heard what seemed to be the voice of a great multitude, like the roar of many waters and like the sound of mighty peals of thunder, crying out, "Hallelujah! For the Lord our God the Almighty reigns. ⁷ Let us rejoice and exult and give him the glory, for the marriage of the Lamb has come, and his Bride has made herself ready; ⁸ it was granted her to clothe herself with fine linen, bright and pure"—for the fine linen is the righteous deeds of the saints. ⁹ And the angel said to me, "Write this: Blessed are those who are invited to the marriage supper of the Lamb." And he said to me, "These are the true words of God."

Matthew 22:30 – For in the resurrection they neither marry nor are given in marriage, but are like angels in heaven.

John 19:34 – But one of the soldiers pierced his side with a spear, and at once there came out blood and water.

The apostle Paul tells us that the purpose for marriage, from the beginning, was Jesus' eternal union with His church. Jesus fulfills marriage by uniting His church to Himself eternally by His Holy Spirit. Just as Eve was created from Adam's rib, we are born again from Christ's bloody side. His finished work, from His Father's election and as applied to us by His Holy Spirit, saves us forever. Through faith in Jesus, we are forever one with Him, to where we are called "the body of Christ" (1 Cor 12:27; Eph 1:22-23; 4:11-12; Col 1:18).

Application

When you lust, you deny that males and females were created by God for marriage, not lust. God designed sex within the covenant of marriage, and any sexual desire outside of this design is the beginning of lust. You should not desire sex outside of marriage. Biblically, it's good to love a woman, to think she's beautiful, to want to marry her, to plan to cut a sexual covenant with her, but to desire to consummate this covenant before it's cut, is sin.

When you lust, you also degrade the value of others, denying that your object needs protection. In the Scriptures, husbands are expected to protect their wives. The apostle Peter wrote, "Likewise, husbands, live with your wives in an understanding way, showing honor to the woman as the weaker vessel, since they are heirs with you of the grace of life, so that your prayers may not be hindered" (1 Pet 3:7). When you look at a woman sexually, and she is not your wife, you are unconcerned about protecting her. If you were concerned about protecting her, you would desire to protect her from men who objectify her, including yourself. Marriage and protection are a result of love and come before sex; and lust comes from hate, preferring yourself above God and the person you're lusting after.

Furthermore, by you lustfully using this woman, not only are you doing the opposite of protecting her, you're using her for sexual immorality without her knowledge, against her will. Some may ask at this point, "What if the woman wants you to lust? If she wants me to lust, then my lust is not against her will?" Just because an image-bearer does not know her value, does not give you the right to disagree with God and agree with her. We ultimately reject lust not because it goes against the will of an image-bearer, but because it goes against God's will.

Now, if you lust after a woman who does not want you to, the sin is more heinous because you are not only violating God's will, but an image-bearer's will as well. Instead, as Paul told Timothy, we should encourage "older women as mothers, younger women as sisters, in all purity" (1 Tim 5:1-2).

Today, will you value God's design above your flesh? Will you value others above yourself and treat them in your heart according to God's design? In the power of the Holy Spirit, you can, but will you?

Marching Orders: Thinking God's Thoughts After Him

Receive, believe, and live the truths you've read. Memorize and meditate on these truths today:

One Sentence to Shape Your Affections:

God designed me as male or female for marriage, with singleness as the exception, to reflect His glory, not for lust.

One Poem to Shape Your Affections:

From Adam's rib, God formed his bride,
A piece of him, no longer in his side.
From his rib removed, Eve came to be,
Both incomplete, longing for their unity.

God joined them together, one flesh to form,
A man leaves his kin, and to his wife is sworn.
In every soul, this truth is spun,
Male and female, created to be one.

Yet Paul praised singleness, a gift rare,
For some to serve God, free from worldly care.
But marriage sings of God's great plan,
His church united in Christ, by the Spirit's hand.

From Jesus' side, blood and water flowed free,
His Spirit given to me, reborn to be.
As Eve from Adam, the church from Christ,
Not for lust, but one flesh through His sacrifice.

One Song to Shape Your Affections:

Add this song to your playlist, "O Love That Will Not Let Me Go."

On YouTube,

By Indelible Grace Music (Written by George Matheson)

https://www.youtube.com/watch?v=Yg4-JJ_UyIU

1. O Love that will not let me go,
I rest my weary soul in thee;
I give thee back the life I owe,
That in thine ocean depths its flow
May richer, fuller be.

2. O light that followest all my way,
I yield my flickering torch to thee;
My heart restores its borrowed ray,
That in thy sunshine's blaze its day
May brighter, fairer be.

3. O Joy that seekest me through pain,
I cannot close my heart to thee;
I trace the rainbow through the rain,
And feel the promise is not vain,
That morn shall tearless be.

4. O Cross that liftest up my head,
I dare not ask to fly from thee;
I lay in dust life's glory dead,
And from the ground there blossoms red
Life that shall endless be.[26]

End with Prayer

---

[26] "O Love That Wilt Not Let Me Go," Hymnary, Accessed September 13, 2025, https://hymnary.org/text/o_love_that_wilt_not_let_me_go.

Day 28

God Created for His Own Glory / Lust Hides God's Glory

Begin with Prayer

Scripture and Reflection

Job 1:6-12 –

> [6] Now there was a day when the sons of God came to present themselves before the LORD, and Satan also came among them. [7] The LORD said to Satan, "From where have you come?" Satan answered the LORD and said, "From going to and fro on the earth, and from walking up and down on it." [8] And the LORD said to Satan, "Have you considered my servant Job, that there is none like him on the earth, a blameless and upright man, who fears God and turns away from evil?" [9] Then Satan answered the LORD and said, "Does Job fear God for no reason? [10] Have you not put a hedge around him and his house and all that he has, on every side? You have blessed the work of his hands, and his possessions have increased in the land. [11] But stretch out your hand and touch all that he has, and he will curse you to your face." [12] And the LORD said to Satan, "Behold, all that he has is in your hand. Only against him do not stretch out your hand." So Satan went out from the presence of the LORD.

In the beginning of the book of Job, Satan told God that Job only worships Him for His gifts. He claimed that Job only feared God because He protected him and blessed his work and possessions. He even said if God took his blessings away,

Job would curse Him to His face. Satan not only slandered Job, but he also demeaned God, by implying that He is only worthy of worship for *what* He gives not for *what* and *who* He *is*.

Proverbs 7:1-5 –

> My son, keep my words and treasure up my commandments with you; [2] keep my commandments and live; keep my teaching as the apple of your eye; [3] bind them on your fingers; write them on the tablet of your heart. [4] Say to wisdom, "You are my sister," and call insight your intimate friend, [5] to keep you from the forbidden woman, from the adulteress with her smooth words.

Solomon tells us that the way to keep from the forbidden woman is to embrace wisdom as our sister and intimate friend. We should view the temptress as an enemy even though she comes with honeyed words of seduction.

Proverbs 7:6-27 –

> [6] For at the window of my house I have looked out through my lattice, [7] and I have seen among the simple, I have perceived among the youths, a young man lacking sense, [8] passing along the street near her corner, taking the road to her house [9] in the twilight, in the evening, at the time of night and darkness. [10] And behold, the woman meets him, dressed as a prostitute, wily of heart. [11] She is loud and wayward; her feet do not stay at home; [12] now in the street, now in the market, and at every corner she lies in wait. [13] She seizes him and kisses him, and with bold face she says to him, [14] "I had to offer sacrifices, and today I have paid my vows; [15] so now I have come out to meet you, to seek you eagerly, and I have found you. [16] I have spread my couch with coverings, colored linens from Egyptian linen; [17] I have perfumed my bed with myrrh, aloes, and cinnamon. [18] Come, let us take our fill of love till morning; let us delight ourselves with love. [19] For my husband is not at home; he has gone on a long journey; [20] he took a bag of money with him; at full moon he will come home."

²¹ With much seductive speech she persuades him; with her smooth talk she compels him. ²² All at once he follows her, as an ox goes to the slaughter, or as a stag is caught fast ²³ till an arrow pierces its liver; as a bird rushes into a snare; he does not know that it will cost him his life. ²⁴ And now, O sons, listen to me, and be attentive to the words of my mouth. ²⁵ Let not your heart turn aside to her ways; do not stray into her paths, ²⁶ for many a victim has she laid low, and all her slain are a mighty throng. ²⁷ Her house is the way to Sheol, going down to the chambers of death.

Solomon says that he's witnessed many young men sneakily travel to the forbidden woman's house, under the cover of night, thinking their sin will go unseen and they'll escape harm. She masquerades as virtuous, boasting of her sacrifices and paid vows. Yet, she seeks to seduce by decorating her bed with expensive linen and fragrances, and she presents the affair in the best possible light, calling it "love" and "delight." But it's all lies, meant to ensnare the weak and foolish; her bed is an open grave. No one visits her and escapes unscathed. She's buried many strong men, but no wise men.

Application

When you lust, you use yourself and someone else in a way that is contrary to God's design. Not only does this speak ill of you and the other person, it speaks ill of God. You've found a better use for God's creation than He intended. Instead of enjoying the beauty of God's design, you've convinced yourself that it's lovelier when twisted, defying God and hiding His glory.

When you lust, you reject wisdom and embrace foolishness, thinking yourself the exception to the millions of murdered men that have gone before you. Lust lulls you to sleep with delusion, and brings you into a drunken stupor, thinking yourself wise when you're immature. On your tombstone, perhaps they'll put, "Here lies _____, the only man to ever survive the adulterous woman." You stand in a grave but dig deeper still.

Wisdom calls you to life and holiness. Will you reject lust and the forbidden woman today, or dig deeper into her grave?

Marching Orders: Thinking God's Thoughts After Him

Receive, believe, and live the truths you've read. Memorize and meditate on these truths today:

One Sentence to Shape Your Affections:

When I use God's creation in a way that twists His design, like lust, I dishonor His glory, claiming my wisdom surpasses His.

One Poem to Shape Your Affections:

Satan mocked Job's worship, not in part,
Said God's blessings alone won his heart.
He sneered, "Job's faith is all for naught,
Strip your gifts, he'll curse You; he's bought."
Not just Job, but God he dared to scorn,
"God's worthy only when His gifts adorn."

Solomon taught, cling to wisdom's hand,
A sister to guide through treacherous land.
For the temptress seduces with honeyed lies,
With "love" and "delight" where every fool dies.
Immature men lust beneath twilight's shade,
Thinking sin's price will never be paid.

Lust twists God's design, in Satan's guile,
Saying, "I'll use God's creation to self-defile."
It scorns God's plan, claiming wiser ways,
Spurning His gifts, mocking Him who saves.
Yet wisdom cries, "Flee the temptress, desire what's right,

Seek life through Christ or dig your grave tonight."

One Song to Shape Your Affections:

Add this song to your playlist, "God, Be Merciful to Me (Psalm 51)"

On YouTube,
By Indelible Grace (Written by Scottish Psalter)

https://www.youtube.com/watch?v=fc3gpwfaLFE

1. God, be merciful to me;
On Thy grace I rest my plea
Plenteous in compassion Thou,
Blot out my transgressions now;
Wash me, make me pure within;
Cleanse, O cleanse me from my sin.

2. My transgressions I confess;
Grief and guilt my soul oppress.
I have sinned against Thy grace,
And provoked Thee to Thy face.
I confess Thy judgement just;
Speechless, I Thy mercy trust.

3. I am evil, born in sin;
Thou desirest truth within.
Thou alone my Savior art,
Teach Thy wisdom to my heart;
Make me pure, Thy grace bestow,
Wash me whiter than the snow.

4. Broken, humbled to the dust
By Thy wrath and judgment just,

Let my contrite heart rejoice,
And in gladness hear Thy voice;
From my sins O hide Thy face,
Blot them out in boundless grace.

5. Gracious God, my heart renew,
Make my spirit right and true.
Cast me not away from Thee,
Let Thy Spirit dwell in me;
Thy salvation's joy impart,
Steadfast make my willing heart.

6. Sinners then shall learn from me,
And return, O God, to Thee
Savior all my guilt remove,
And my tongue shall sing Thy love
Touch my silent lips, O Lord,
And my mouth shall praise accord.[27]

End with Prayer

[27] "God, Be Merciful to Me," Hymnary, Accessed September 13, 2025,
https://hymnary.org/text/god_be_merciful_to_me_on_thy_grace.

Day 29

Christ's Beauty Destroys Idols / Lust Creates Them

Begin with Prayer

Scripture and Reflection

Mark 14:26-31 –

[After the Last Supper,] 26 And when they had sung a hymn, they went out to the Mount of Olives. 27 And Jesus said to them, "You will all fall away, for it is written, 'I will strike the shepherd, and the sheep will be scattered' [Zech 13:7]. 28 But after I am raised up, I will go before you to Galilee." 29 Peter said to him, "Even though they all fall away, I will not." 30 And Jesus said to him, "Truly, I tell you, this very night, before the rooster crows twice, you will deny me three times." 31 But he said emphatically, "If I must die with you, I will not deny you." And they all said the same.

Peter boldly vowed to remain faithful to Jesus to the end, yet within hours of declaring, "Even though they all fall away, I will not," he denied being Christ's disciple three times. His failure stemmed from trusting himself over Jesus, whose words are always true and beyond correction.

Matthew 26:69-75 –

69 Now Peter was sitting outside in the courtyard. And a servant girl came up to him and said, "You also were with Jesus the Galilean." 70 But he denied it

before them all, saying, "I do not know what you mean." ⁷¹ And when he went out to the entrance, another servant girl saw him, and she said to the bystanders, "This man was with Jesus of Nazareth." ⁷² And again he denied it with an oath: "I do not know the man." ⁷³ After a little while the bystanders came up and said to Peter, "Certainly you too are one of them, for your accent betrays you." ⁷⁴ Then he began to invoke a curse on himself and to swear, "I do not know the man." And immediately the rooster crowed. ⁷⁵ And Peter remembered the saying of Jesus, "Before the rooster crows, you will deny me three times." And he went out and wept bitterly.

Luke 22:61-62 – ⁶¹ And the Lord turned and looked at Peter. And Peter remembered the saying of the Lord, how he had said to him, "Before the rooster crows today, you will deny me three times." ⁶² And he went out and wept bitterly.

Peter first denied Jesus to a servant of the High Priest, then before bystanders, appealing to God as his witness with an oath, taking His name in vain by associating Him with a bold lie. An hour later (Luke 22:59), he denied Christ again, cursing himself, essentially saying, "If I'm lying, may God kill me and send me to hell." Peter's sin grew worse with each denial. But then, Jesus looked at him, and though He stood arrested and condemned, the beauty of Christ, His perfect holiness and love, melted Peter's heart. How could he possibly deny His Savior and Lord who had never done him any wrong, only good?! Overwhelmed, Peter fled and wept bitterly.

John 21:15-19 –

[After Jesus died and rose from the dead, He came to Peter.] ¹⁵ When they had finished breakfast, Jesus said to Simon Peter, "Simon, son of John, do you love me more than these?" He said to him, "Yes, Lord; you know that I love you." He said to him, "Feed my lambs." ¹⁶ He said to him a second time, "Simon, son of John, do you love me?" He said to him, "Yes, Lord; you know that I love you." He said to him, "Tend my sheep." ¹⁷ He said to him the third time, "Simon, son of John, do you love me?" Peter was grieved because he said to him the third time, "Do you love me?" and he said to him,

"Lord, you know everything; you know that I love you." Jesus said to him, "Feed my sheep. [18] Truly, truly, I say to you, when you were young, you used to dress yourself and walk wherever you wanted, but when you are old, you will stretch out your hands, and another will dress you and carry you where you do not want to go." [19] (This he said to show by what kind of death he was to glorify God.) And after saying this he said to him, "Follow me."

Hebrews 12:1-2 –

Therefore, since we are surrounded by so great a cloud of witnesses, let us also lay aside every weight, and sin which clings so closely, and let us run with endurance the race that is set before us, [2] looking to Jesus, the founder and perfecter of our faith, who for the joy that was set before him endured the cross, despising the shame, and is seated at the right hand of the throne of God.

If Peter truly loves Jesus, he must live that love by feeding His lambs, tending His sheep, and feeding His sheep. It's not enough to pledge devotion to Christ, Peter must do what Jesus says. When Jesus asks Peter, "Do you love me?" twice, He uses the Greek word, "agapaó," signifying unconditional love. Peter replies with the Greek word "phileó," expressing his deep brotherly love for Jesus. Then, the third time, Jesus uses the word that Peter had been using, phileó, essentially asking, "Do you *really* love Me, Peter, in the way that you claim?" Grieved, Peter declares, "Lord, you know everything; you know that I love you." Finally, Jesus tells Peter that he will persevere as His disciple, but it will cost him his life.

In a similar fashion to Peter looking to Jesus, the author of Hebrews tells us, because of all those who came before who trusted in the coming Christ, we too must lay aside sin and look to Jesus, running with endurance the race of Christianity that is set before us.

Application

When you lust, you deceive yourself, and the more you give yourself to it, the more time and devotion, and dare I say, the more you love it, the more you deny

Christ. If you've given yourself to lust often, you've probably found that your sin has grown worse, your conscience has gotten quieter, and you struggle to see Christ's beauty like you once did. Like Peter, you must see Christ looking at you, and think, "How can I possibly deny Jesus through lust, the holy One, He who is love, and deny His word, which is absolutely true?" Weeping bitterly should be your natural response to seeing Christ looking at you. So now, run to Him, embrace Him, and live His commands.

Christ's beauty and His love for you, and your love for Him, must compel you to repent of your lust at the root. If you give the time and devotion to Christ that you once gave to lust, you'll find your appreciation of His beauty increasing. He stays the same, but our love grows or decreases, and if you have a lust problem, you have a love for Jesus problem. Repent of lust at the root and cultivate love for Jesus by enjoying His beauty above all until you find your lust so ugly that you can't possibly fathom how you could give your affections to it.

Christ's beauty is supreme because He is of infinite worth. Today, will you see, focus on, and aim at the supreme worth of Christ? If so, you'll give your affections to Him, hate any form of lust that springs up in your flesh, and enjoy the freedom from sin that only He provides.

Marching Orders: Thinking God's Thoughts After Him

Receive, believe, and live the truths you've read. Memorize and meditate on these truths today:

One Sentence to Shape Your Affections:

Christ, God the Son in the flesh, is the most beautiful of all creation, and sees me and draws me to love and enjoy Him above all things, for He is of infinite worth, and exposes lust as worthless.

One Poem to Shape Your Affections:

Peter vowed to stand, faithful to the end,

Yet denied Christ thrice, submitting to sin.
Trusting himself, not Jesus, he lied with haste,
"I do not know Him," each with more distaste.

First to a servant, then with an oath profane,
Using God's name in vain, a more heinous stain.
An hour later, curses extended his shame,
But Christ pierced the dark, sparking holy flame.

How could he deny such perfect love?
His heart turned, and tears fell like a dove.
"Feed My lambs, tend My sheep," hear Christ call,
Love Him in heart, soul, and mind, stand tall.

See Christ gaze, weep and run to His side,
Where infinite love and blessings abide.
For lust trades Beauty for blight,
But repentance trades darkness for Light.

One Song to Shape Your Affections:

Add this song to your playlist, "Abide With Me."

On YouTube,
By Indelible Grace Music (Written by Henry Lyte and Justin Smith)

https://www.youtube.com/watch?v=PdqA0eO7PWs

1. Abide with me; falls the eventide;
The darkness deepens; Lord with me abide.
When other helpers, fail and comforts flee,
Help of the helpless, abide with me.

2. Thou on my head, in early youth didst smile;
And, though rebellious, and perverse meanwhile,
Thou hast not left me, though I oft left Thee,
On to the close Lord, abide with me.

3. I need Thy presence, every passing hour.
What but Thy grace, can foil the tempter's power?
Who, like Thyself, my guide and stay can be?
Through cloud and sunshine, abide with me.

4. I fear no foe, with Thee at hand to bless
Ills have no weight, tears lose their bitterness
Where is thy sting death? Where grave thy victory?
I triumph still, abide with me.

5. Hold Thou Thy cross, before my closing eyes;
Shine through the gloom, and point me to the skies.
Heaven's morning breaks, and earth's vain shadows flee;
In life, in death, Lord, abide with me.[28]

End with Prayer

---

[28] "Abide With Me," Hymnary, Accessed September 13, 2025, https://hymnary.org/text/abide_with_me_fast_falls_the_eventide.

Day 30

Christle is our Identity / Lust is our Enemy

Begin with Prayer

Scripture and Reflection

1 Thessalonians 4:1-8 –

> Finally, then, brothers, we ask and urge you in the Lord Jesus, that as
> you received from us how you ought to walk and to please God, just as you
> are doing, that you do so more and more. ² For you know what instructions
> we gave you through the Lord Jesus. ³ For this is the will of God, your
> sanctification: that you abstain from sexual immorality; ⁴ that each one of you
> know how to control his own body in holiness and honor, ⁵ not in the
> passion of lust like the Gentiles who do not know God; ⁶ that no one
> transgress and wrong his brother in this matter, because the Lord is an
> avenger in all these things, as we told you beforehand and solemnly warned
> you. ⁷ For God has not called us for impurity, but in holiness. ⁸ Therefore
> whoever disregards this, disregards not man but God, who gives his Holy
> Spirit to you.

Paul commended the Thessalonian Christians for their holiness, but he did not
want them to become complacent. Instead, he encouraged them to pursue
holiness more and more. God's will for Christians is clear: to be set apart from
the sexual immorality in the world through sanctification. Unlike those who do
not know God and are driven by lustful passions, believers are called to exercise

self-control, honoring God with our bodies. We must train ourselves to live and believe that it is *unbelievers* who are sexually immoral, *not* Christians. We belong body and soul to God and are united to Christ, not the world.

1 Thessalonians 4:6-7 – ⁶ that no one transgress and wrong his brother in this matter, because the Lord is an avenger in all these things, as we told you beforehand and solemnly warned you. ⁷ For God has not called us for impurity, but in holiness.

Like a boy who talks back to his mother, and his dad overhears and walks into the room, we too, as God's children, should have a healthy fear of Him. This isn't a fear of Him abandoning us or breaking His promises to us, but a healthy fear of His discipline. There is a judgment day coming when everything that we did in secret will be revealed and judged. Those who are in Christ will rule and reign with Him in a new heavens and new earth forever, but we may suffer loss of reward due to how we lived here on earth (2 Cor 5:9-10). For, God has not called us in impurity of heart, but in holiness, to be like Jesus in both thought and deed.

2 Timothy 2:22 – So flee youthful passions and pursue righteousness, faith, love, and peace, along with those who call on the Lord from a pure heart.

In his final letter to Timothy, Paul urged believers to flee youthful passions, like lust, which can derail a Christian's life. Instead of chasing lustful desires, run from them, and pursue a life that reflects Christ's heart:

1) Moral uprightness.
2) Faith in the Trinity.
3) Love for God and others.
4) Peace with God and others.

Through the Holy Spirit's purifying work in us, our hearts are transformed, and we are empowered to repent of lust at the root and live godly lives.

1 Peter 1:13-16 –

> [Because the gospel has been faithfully preached to us, and we have believed,]
> 13 Therefore, preparing your minds for action, and being sober-minded, set your hope fully on the grace that will be brought to you at the revelation of Jesus Christ. 14 As obedient children, do not be conformed to the passions of your former ignorance, 15 but as he who called you is holy, you also be holy in all your conduct, 16 since it is written, "You shall be holy, for I am holy."

Because God has graciously provided our salvation, we are called to live with purpose, preparing our minds for action by reading, receiving, and believing His word. We must be sober-minded, consistent thinkers and emotionally stable, not flying from one extreme to the next. As God's obedient children, we must leave our past lives in the past. Leave behind the sins that you committed in ignorance, when you didn't understand who Christ was and the supreme value of God.

We have a new identity in Christ, publicly declared through baptism in the "Name," singular, of the "Father, Son, and Holy Spirit," plural (Matt 28:18-20). Through baptism, we publicly identify with the One God (name) who eternally exists in three distinct Persons. As Leviticus 11:44 says, "Be holy, for I am holy," God expects all those associated with His name to be holy. Through Christ, God has declared us holy (salvation/sanctification), is making us holy (progressive sanctification), and will make us completely holy in the new heavens and new earth (glorification); therefore, we must live holy lives that reflect Him.

1 Peter 1:17-21 –

> 17 And if you call on him as Father who judges impartially according to each one's deeds, conduct yourselves with fear throughout the time of your exile, 18 knowing that you were ransomed from the futile ways inherited from your forefathers, not with perishable things such as silver or gold, 19 but with the precious blood of Christ, like that of a lamb without blemish or spot. 20 He was foreknown before the foundation of the world but was made manifest in the last times for the sake of you 21 who through him are believers in God,

who raised him from the dead and gave him glory, so that your faith and hope are in God.

Since we pray to God as our Father, we must live like this world is not our home, because it isn't. God is just and He will soon balance the books. No one gets away with anything in all creation, for God's judgment always comes and is always perfect. As Christians, we should have a healthy fear of God. We should fear His discipline, while never fearing His condemnation. For, in Christ, we are now under "no condemnation" (Rom 8:1) and never will be.

We must know that in Christ, our salvation was secured not with fleeting treasures like silver or gold, but with the precious blood of Christ. He is the spotless Lamb. Before the world's foundation, God chose to save us through Christ's sacrifice.

God is never "flying by the seat of His pants." Although, man is free to act and do according to his nature, God is in control of all things. Everything is predetermined by God, either directly (good) or indirectly (evil). Whatever our God ordains is right, and evil serves His greater glory. This reality should comfort us. For, God is all-powerful, all-knowing, and all-good. That's who you want to be in control. Through belief in Christ, we are believers in God. He has raised Christ from the dead, giving him glory for His perfect desires and works, so that our faith and hope are in God.

Application

When you lust, you are pulled back to the life that Christ saved you from; a life of shame that brought you to Christ to begin with. Lust has no value, so give it its due, which is nothing. Treat Christ as priceless and lust as worthless.

When you lust, you heed your flesh and the devil's lie, "you will not surely die!" Yet only dead men call you to embrace what kills; and only the One who rose from the dead and still lives today forevermore, Christ Jesus, calls you to life in Him and His righteousness.

When you lust, you stunt your growth in Christ, for lust brings continual spiritual infancy. How can you possibly grow and mature in the mire where pigs wallow? Having been cleansed by Christ, don't return to the world. Give lust no quarter in your life.

When you lust, you desire as if your identity is in your flesh not Christ. You were not baptized in the name of lust or of yourself. You were baptized in the Name of the Father, Son, and Holy Spirit, so that you would live for Him alone.

Today, will you remember why you came to Christ to be begin with? The world has nothing for you. Christ is your Lord, your identity is in Him, and your flesh and the devil are your enemies. Will you pursue maturity in Christ by forsaking lust and living His righteousness? You can, but will you?

Marching Orders: Thinking God's Thoughts After Him

Receive, believe, and live the truths you've read. Memorize and meditate on these truths today:

One Sentence to Shape Your Affections:

Christ is my identity; therefore, God calls me to flee lust and to live for Him, empowered by His Holy Spirit to live a redeemed life.

One Poem to Shape Your Affections:

Strive for holiness, Christ's chosen kin,
Like Paul, do not let complacency win.
Set apart from lust, the world's dark sway,
Control your body, desire faith's bright way.

Fear God's discipline, though it's His love's embrace,
For His correction comes to eliminate sin's every trace.
In Christ, heaven's sure, but rewards may suffer loss,

Live pure in heart and deed, like Jesus, not dross.

Run from youth's passions, as Timothy did learn,
Pursue righteousness and peace, where love's fires burn.
Sober mind, leave old sins behind, once your shame,
Now, baptized in the Name, and not your own fame.

Fear God not man, and not the mirror,
For your identity is Christ, so see Him clearer.
Called not to impurity, but holy obscurity,
The blood of Jesus, your all, your only surety.

One Song Often to Shape Your Affections:

Add this song to your playlist, "Jesus I Come."

On YouTube,
By Sovereign Grace Music (Written by William True Sleeper)

https://www.youtube.com/watch?v=WSoer0VicaA

1. Out of my bondage, sorrow and night,
Jesus, I come; Jesus I come.
Into Thy freedom, gladness and light,
Jesus, I come to Thee.
Out of my sickness into Thy health,
Out of my wanting and into Thy wealth,
Out of my sin and into Thyself,
Jesus, I come to Thee.

2. Out of my shameful failure and loss,
Jesus, I come; Jesus, I come.
Into the glorious gain of Thy cross,
Jesus, I come to Thee.

Out of earth's sorrows into Thy balm,
Out of life's storms and into Thy calm,
Out of distress into jubilant psalm,
Jesus, I come to Thee.

3. Out of unrest and arrogant pride,
Jesus, I come; Jesus, I come.
Into Thy blessed will to abide,
Jesus, I come to Thee.
Out of myself to dwell in Thy love,
Out of despair into raptures above,
Upward forever on wings like a dove,
Jesus, I come to Thee.

4. Out of the fear and dread of the tomb,
Jesus, I come; Jesus, I come.
Into the joy and light of Thy home,
Jesus, I come to Thee.
Out of the depths of ruin untold,
Into the peace of Thy sheltering fold,
Ever Thy glorious face to behold,
Jesus, I come to Thee.[29]

End with Prayer

---

[29] "Jesus, I Come," Hymnary, September 13, 2025,
https://hymnary.org/text/out_of_my_bondage_sorrow_and_night.

Day 31

Holiness is From Above / Lust is From Below

Begin with Prayer

Scripture and Reflection

<u>Genesis 3:6</u> – When the woman saw that the fruit of the tree was good for food and pleasing to the eye, and also desirable for gaining wisdom, she took some and ate it. She also gave some to her husband, who was with her, and he ate it.

<u>Deuteronomy 5:21</u> – "'And you shall not covet your neighbor's wife. And you shall not desire your neighbor's house, his field, or his male servant, or his female servant, his ox, or his donkey, or anything that is your neighbor's.'

Once Eve viewed the forbidden tree through the serpent's eyes, she began desiring and thinking like him. The Hebrew word translated "desirable" is the same word translated "covet" in the 10th Commandment. Eve coveted the forbidden tree, twisting God's good creation. She willed sin in her heart, then ate with her mouth, and immediately tempted her husband, like the serpent.

This reveals a sobering truth: lust begins not as a neutral impulse but as sin's seed, bearing the same evil nature from its first impulse to its bitter end. Not only can you not commit sexual immorality, but you also can't desire it in any form, not even in your heart, not even a fleeting thought, impulse, inclination, or desire.

James 1:13-18 –

[After telling his hearers that God gives us trials to mature us (James 1:2-4), he writes,] ¹³ Let no one say when he is tempted, "I am being tempted by God," for God cannot be tempted with evil, and he himself tempts no one. ¹⁴ But each person is tempted when he is lured and enticed by his own desire. ¹⁵ Then desire when it has conceived gives birth to sin, and sin when it is fully grown brings forth death. ¹⁶ Do not be deceived, my beloved brothers. ¹⁷ Every good gift and every perfect gift is from above, coming down from the Father of lights, with whom there is no variation or shadow due to change. ¹⁸ Of his own will he brought us forth by the word of truth, that we should be a kind of firstfruits of his creatures.

God gives us trials to produce perseverance, to mature and complete us (James 1:2-4), but He never tempts us with evil. He cannot be tempted by sin and can never tempt anyone with sin. Rather, often during our trials, our lusts seize moments of weakness to tempt us with evil. We tempt ourselves. The Greek word translated "desire" (James 1:14) can be translated as good desire or evil desire depending on the context. The context here requires it to be translated as "lust" or "lawless desire" because it's a desire that God cannot produce and it only conceives sin and grows into death (James 1:13-15).

Sin's lifecycle begins in the heart, where our lust lures us like a predator stalking its prey. If the devil tempts us, he sins; if someone tempts us, he or she sins; if we tempt others, we sin; but we also sin when we tempt ourselves.

Then, when we submit to our lusts, our internal temptations, we conceive mindful sin, a deeper form of sin. Had we repented at the first lustful impulse by turning to Christ and confessing the impulse as sin, we could have rejoiced over our repentance and that we didn't go further into sin.

Just as a thornbush yields only thorns, lust can only lure and entice us to mindful sin and death, only producing evil, never anything neutral or good. Though trials come from God for our good, temptation, inner or outer, never does, because He only gives good and perfect gifts. Therefore, our inner lusts are always our fault, never God's; but in the power of the Holy Spirit, we can repent.

James 4:1-4 –

> What causes fights and quarrels among you? Don't they come from your desires that battle within you? ² You desire but do not have, so you kill. You covet but you cannot get what you want, so you quarrel and fight. You do not have because you do not ask God. ³ When you ask, you do not receive, because you ask with wrong motives, that you may spend what you get on your pleasures. ⁴ You adulterous people, don't you know that friendship with the world means enmity against God? Therefore, anyone who chooses to be a friend of the world becomes an enemy of God.

James exposes his hearers' hearts. They have harmed one another, evidently some had even fought and murdered one another. Like a fire unchecked, their lust for what they cannot have sparks fights and divisions (James 4:1-2). Their selfish cravings not only poison their local church but taint their prayers, rendering them ineffective. By chasing their fleeting lusts, they oppose God directly, becoming His adversaries (James 4:3-4).

James 4:7-10 –

> ⁷ Submit yourselves therefore to God. Resist the devil, and he will flee from you. ⁸ Draw near to God, and he will draw near to you. Cleanse your hands, you sinners, and purify your hearts, you double-minded. ⁹ Be wretched and mourn and weep. Let your laughter be turned to mourning and your joy to gloom. ¹⁰ Humble yourselves before the Lord, and he will exalt you.

James calls his hearers to repentance. If they submit to God and resist the devil, he will flee from them. If they draw near to God, He will draw near to them with grace. They must grieve over their sin, turning laughter to tears and joy to sorrow, for they have wallowed in rebellion. Like a millstone, their sin must weigh upon their hearts until, humbled before the Lord, they confess and turn from it. Then, He will lift them up, restoring them in His mercy (James 4:7-10).

Application

Lust begins as an evil impulse in your heart, tempting you to commit mindful sexual immorality. It's not a fleeting thought but a sin to uproot through repentance before it spreads, harming you and others. Confess it as sin, turn to Christ, and rejoice in His grace that frees you.

When you lust, you reveal your adulterous heart. Only adulterous hearts lust. Hate your sin like God does, weep and mourn over it, and draw near to Him and He will draw near to you. If married, pursue your spouse sexually. If single and burning with passion, find the godliest opposite sex Christian you can, and marry, as Scripture commands (1 Cor 7:8-9). If you're burning with passion, you don't have the gift of singleness.

Will you repent of your lust at the root today? Will you name every lustful impulse as sin, reject it, and delight in Christ above all? By the Holy Spirit's power, you can, but will you?

Marching Orders: Thinking God's Thoughts After Him

Receive, believe, and live the truths you've read. Memorize and meditate on these truths today:

One Sentence to Shape Your Affections:

I am responsible for every evil impulse that springs up in my heart, including lust, and by the Holy Spirit's power within me, I can repent and pursue loving God with all my heart, soul, and mind.

One Poem to Shape Your Affections:

In Eden's lush beauty, Eve denied her duty,
Through serpent eyes, she called evil, beauty.
She coveted as wise what God forbade,
Her lust took root, her heart betrayed.

No spark of lust is free from guilt,
Root and fruit require my blood to be spilt.
God's trials mature me, but never entice,
My lust alone breeds sin's dark vice.

I tempt myself, my heart deceives,
I lay with the devil, and sin conceives.
Unrepentance feeds lust until it grows to death,
A leech sucking precious years of fleeting breath.

Repent of lust at the root, confess the sin,
Turn to Christ, His grace will win.
Mourn your lust, trade joy for pain,
Humble yourself, God's mercy is gain.

Adulterous hearts chase worldly lust,
Their prayers falter, they're enthralled by dust.
Submit to God, and resist the foe,
Draw near to Him, and His commands will sow.

Before lust consumes, pursue what's right,
A godly spouse, a covenant bright.
Flee from sin, embrace God's call,
Repent, rejoice, and pursue Christ, your all.

One Song to Shape Your Affections:

Add this song to your playlist, "Thy Mercy My God."

On YouTube,
By Indelible Grace (Written by John Stocker)

https://www.youtube.com/watch?v=uzRhzk-IY90

1. Thy mercy, my God, is the theme of my song,
The joy of my heart. and the boast of my tongue;
Thy free grace alone, from the first to the last,
Hath won my affections, and bound my soul fast.

2. Without Thy sweet mercy I could not live here;
Sin would reduce me to utter despair;
But, through Thy free goodness, my spirits revive,
And He that first made me still keeps me alive.

3. Thy mercy is more than a match for my heart,
Which wonders to feel its own hardness depart;
Dissolved by Thy goodness, I fall to the ground,
And weep to the praise of the mercy I've found.

4. Great Father of mercies, Thy goodness I own,
And the covenant love of Thy crucified Son;
All praise to the Spirit, Whose whisper divine
Seals mercy, and pardon, and righteousness mine.
All praise to the Spirit, Whose whisper divine
Seals mercy, and pardon, and righteousness mine.[30]

End with Prayer

---

[30] "Thy Mercy My God," Indelible Grace Hymn Book, September 13, 2025, http://hymnbook.igracemusic.com/hymns/thy-mercy-my-god.

Day 32

God Empowers us to Live Fruitful Christian Lives / Lust Stunts our Growth in Christ

Begin with Prayer

Scripture and Reflection

Psalm 104:24-30 –

> [24] O Lord, how manifold are your works! In wisdom have you made them all; the earth is full of your creatures. [25] Here is the sea, great and wide, which teems with creatures innumerable, living things both small and great. [26] There go the ships, and Leviathan, which you formed to play in it. [27] These all look to you, to give them their food in due season. [28] When you give it to them, they gather it up; when you open your hand, they are filled with good things. [29] When you hide your face, they are dismayed; when you take away their breath, they die and return to their dust. [30] When you send forth your Spirit, they are created, and you renew the face of the ground.

2 Peter 1:3-4 –

> [3] His divine power has granted to us all things that pertain to life and godliness, through the knowledge of him who called us to his own glory and excellence, [4] by which he has granted to us his precious and very great promises, so that through them you may become partakers of the divine nature, having escaped from the corruption that is in the world because of sinful desire.

All that is good, true, and beautiful in our lives comes from God, who generously gives His gifts through His Holy Spirit in both creation and redemption. As Psalm 104:24-30 declares, God's wisdom fills the earth with His creatures, created and sustained by His Spirit. Yet, through the gospel, He has drawn us into deeper relationship with Him, uniting us to Christ by His Spirit through faith. We know God in a way the world does not, for He has called us to be especially associated with His glory and moral excellence. By His Spirit, He has given us His word and enabled us to believe and understand it, by which we know and understand Him.

Peter says that we partake of the Divine Nature, which doesn't mean theosis, that we are deified, or that we become one with God's Divine Nature, either. Rather, we have been united with God's Divine Nature because we are united to Jesus, and He is God the Son, the second Person of the Trinity, in the flesh. We are united to Him through His human nature, and He is truly God, truly Divine. By the Holy Spirit uniting us with the Divine Son through His human nature, we partake of God's Divine Nature.

Through union with Christ, we have been freed from the worldly corruption of our own sinful desire, which once enslaved us to the evil of the world. The Holy Spirit has freed our wills from having to submit to our flesh, and He has given us a new nature that loves God, Christ, His Holy Spirit, and His word and morals. We do not have to walk in the flesh because we have been empowered to walk in the Spirit.

2 Peter 1:5-8 –

> 5 For this very reason, make every effort to supplement your faith with virtue, and virtue with knowledge, 6 and knowledge with self-control, and self-control with steadfastness, and steadfastness with godliness, 7 and godliness with brotherly affection, and brotherly affection with love. 8 For if these qualities are yours and are increasing, they keep you from being ineffective or unfruitful in the knowledge of our Lord Jesus Christ.

Because of all the good, truth, and beauty that we have received from God, through Christ, by His Holy Spirit, we are called to reflect His holiness. As 2 Peter

1:5-7 tells us, we must intentionally build upon our faith in Christ, cultivating and adding virtues that make us fruitful in His hand. Empowered by the Spirit, we are to add and increase in,

1) Faith in Christ.
2) Virtue or moral excellence.
3) God's knowledge through His word.
4) Self-control of our evil impulses or desires.
5) Perseverance in faith and morals.
6) Godliness, reflecting God's morals back to Him.
7) Brotherly affection.
8) Love for God and others.

If we lack any of these virtues, we must take responsibility and nurture them through worshiping God with other believers in a local church and in our daily lives. For if we have these qualities and we increase in them, we will never falter. Too many godly men and women have fallen. And every one of them did so because they either lacked these virtues or they did not cultivate them and add them to their faith in Christ. If you want to be an effective Christian in the hand of God, you must possess these qualities and increase in them.

2 Peter 1:9-11 –

⁹ For whoever lacks these qualities is so nearsighted that he is blind, having forgotten that he was cleansed from his former sins. ¹⁰ Therefore, brothers, be all the more diligent to confirm your calling and election, for if you practice these qualities you will never fall. ¹¹ For in this way there will be richly provided for you an entrance into the eternal kingdom of our Lord and Savior Jesus Christ.

Lacking these qualities or not increasing in them means that you've already had a great fall, it's just not public yet. Peter says those who lack these qualities are blind; they have spiritual amnesia, essentially forgetting who they are in Christ and all that He has done for them. They're so near-sighted that they merely live their lives waiting for God to give them more, not even realizing that they have neglected His word, His commands, and His morals. The error is their lack of discipline, for God has empowered them to live marvelously for His glory.

Peter warns us that we must make sure that we have been chosen by God, by producing the fruit of Christ through living out the work the Holy Spirit is doing within our hearts. For, if you practice these eight qualities, "faith, virtue, knowledge, self-control, steadfastness, godliness, brotherly affection, and love," you will never fall. And you'll be confident that you're headed to the eternal kingdom of our Lord and Savior Jesus Christ, because His work is so evident in your life.

Application

When you lust, you render yourself an ineffective Christian, at best. At worst, if unrepentant, you may reveal that you're an unbeliever. A lustful Christian is someone who uses his mind and the bodies of others in ways that are contrary to God's design. If you'll objectify someone in private, you'll use them and others selfishly in public as well. Though we may hide our sin in private, lust shapes our hearts, seeping into our relationships through selfishness, disrespect, and broken trust. You cannot compartmentalize devaluing yourself and others. No one is a different person in public than in private; one will seep into the other. Lust, unaddressed, will hinder your ability to love others as Christ commands.

When you lust, you're adding to your faith sinful desires that hinder it. If you take the effort you once gave to pursuing lust and put it to adding these eight virtues—faith, virtue, knowledge, self-control, steadfastness, godliness, brotherly affection, and love—you will cease from mindful lust, and eventually, lustful impulses. By the Holy Spirit's work, you will mortify your fleshly desires (Rom 8:13; Col 3:5).

All believers remain sinners in this life (1 John 1:8-10), but we are not bound to desire the same sins for the rest of our lives. Though you are declared righteous in Christ through faith because you have been credited with His righteousness, you are still a sinner because you have not been made completely righteous yet.

Your sanctification is not completed until you leave this earth, go to Heaven, and then rule and reign with Christ in your resurrected body in the New Heavens and New Earth. Yet, in this life, by the Holy Spirit, you can put to death particular motions of original sin, like lust or any other sin.

Today, will you diligently repent of your lust at the root and add these virtues to your faith in Christ? Will you live Christ's fruit from your heart? If so, you'll be effective for Christ. By His Spirit, you can, but will you?

Marching Orders: Thinking God's Thoughts After Him

Receive, believe, and live the truths you've read. Memorize and meditate on these truths today:

One Sentence to Shape Your Affections:

By His Spirit through Christ, God has saved me and empowered me to add and increase in His virtues, not lust, gradually maturing me in Christ until He completes in eternity what He started in me.

One Poem to Shape Your Affections:

From God flows all good, truth, and beauty,
He sends His Spirit to produce life and duty.
He unites us to Christ, His glory to show,
By grace, His word, our hearts truly know.

No god am I, yet a partaker of His Nature Divine,
United to the God Man, as a branch to the Vine.
He gives me a new heart; in Him I'm born again,
Idols torn, by the Spirit's power, I'm freed from sin.

Increase in faith, add virtue, then knowledge seek,

To Self-control, add perseverance, aim at the Peak.
Add godliness, brotherly affection, and love abounding,
These guard my heart from Satan's relentless hounding.

Lacking these qualities, I'm blind, I fall,
Quickly forgetting Christ's work, who paid it all.
But increasing in these virtues, firm I'll stand,
Held fast within God's sovereign hand.

But if lust clouds my mind, my witness will fade,
Sin causes love for God and others to degrade.
Turn, repent, pursue the Spirit's fruit,
Put your sin to death, kill its root.

By grace, these virtues I must pursue,
Take responsibility, embrace what's true.
In Christ, I can stand, effective, free,
For God's glory, not my own, eternally.

One Song to Shape Your Affections:

Add this song to your playlist, "The Love of Christ is Rich and Free."

On YouTube,
By Sandra McCracken (Written by William Gadsby)

https://www.youtube.com/watch?v=vZe9B6N4ZVk

1. The love of Christ is rich and free;
Fixed on His own eternally;
Nor earth, nor hell, can it remove;
Long as He lives, His own He'll love.

2. His loving heart engaged to be
Their everlasting Surety;
Twas love that took their cause in hand,
And love maintains it to the end.

3. Love cannot from its post withdraw;
Nor death, nor hell, nor sin, nor law,
Can turn the Surety's heart away;
He'll love His own to endless day.

4. Love has redeemed His sheep with blood;
And love will bring them safe to God;
Love calls them all from death to life;
And love will finish all their strife.

5. He loves through every changing scene,
Nor aught from Him can Zion wean;
Not all the wanderings of her heart
Can make His love for her depart.

6. At death, beyond the grave, He'll love;
In endless bliss, His own shall prove
The blazing glory of that love
Which never could from them remove.[31]

End with Prayer

---

[31] "The Love of Christ is Rich and Free," Hymnary, Accessed September 13, 2025, https://hymnary.org/text/the_love_of_christ_is_rich_and_free.

Day 33

God's Image-Bearers can Only be Satisfied in Him / Lust can Never Satisfy

Begin with Prayer

Scripture and Reflection

Ephesians 5:3-6 –

> ³ But sexual immorality and all impurity or covetousness must not even be named among you, as is proper among saints. ⁴ Let there be no filthiness nor foolish talk nor crude joking, which are out of place, but instead let there be thanksgiving. ⁵ For you may be sure of this, that everyone who is sexually immoral or impure, or who is covetous (that is, an idolater), has no inheritance in the kingdom of Christ and God. ⁶ Let no one deceive you with empty words, for because of these things the wrath of God comes upon the sons of disobedience.

Impurity or covetousness refers to a state of any form of lust or sexual immorality. It shouldn't even be named among Christians. This includes homosexuality or same-sex attraction, for these are the root of lust, produced by the flesh not the Spirit.

Paul says the remedy for lust is thanksgiving. Why? Because jealousy and discontentment are inherent in lust. To lust, you must not be thankful for God. You're jealous of Him, thinking you know better and have better use for creation than He designed. You're also discontent with what God has given you in this life. If you're married, you're not thankful for your spouse, so you lust. If you're single, you're not thankful for the singleness God has given you, so you lust.

The remedy is to be satisfied with God and His providence. If you're thankful, you won't lust. If you lack thankfulness, you must cultivate it through,

1) Worshipping God with other Christians in a local church.
2) Hearing, reading, believing, singing, and meditating on His word.
3) Praying to Him in faith.

His beauty is of infinite worth, and He created us; therefore, we should be satisfied with Him. Our gratitude for Him should never cease or decrease, and we should know that reflecting His image is the greatest good we could possibly pursue.

Colossians 3:1-10 –

If then you have been raised with Christ, seek the things that are above, where Christ is, seated at the right hand of God. [2] Set your minds on things that are above, not on things that are on earth. [3] For you have died, and your life is hidden with Christ in God. [4] When Christ who is your life appears, then you also will appear with him in glory. [5] Put to death therefore what is earthly in you: sexual immorality, impurity, passion, evil desire, and covetousness, which is idolatry. [6] On account of these the wrath of God is coming. [7] In these you too once walked, when you were living in them. [8] But now you must put them all away: anger, wrath, malice, slander, and obscene talk from your mouth. [9] Do not lie to one another, seeing that you have put off the old self with its practices [10] and have put on the new self, which is being renewed in knowledge after the image of its creator.

Romans 8:12-13 – [12] So then, brothers, we are debtors, not to the flesh, to live according to the flesh. [13] For if you live according to the flesh you will die, but if by the Spirit you put to death the deeds of the body, you will live.

Romans 12:1-2 –

> I appeal to you therefore, brothers, by the mercies of God, to present your bodies as a living sacrifice, holy and acceptable to God, which is your spiritual worship. ²Do not be conformed to this world, but be transformed by the renewal of your mind, that by testing you may discern what is the will of God, what is good and acceptable and perfect.

Having been raised with Christ, we must long to be in Heaven with Him. We must set our minds on Him and the eternal life He has provided for us. We have died with Christ and have been raised to life in Him, that where He is, we may be also. When He returns, we will also be with Him in glory. This glorious truth should shape our affections in such a way that lust becomes unthinkable to us, something that is beneath us. It's part of the old man, not the new one who has been born again in Christ.

Because we're united to Christ in His death, resurrection, ascension, and exaltation, we must put to death what is fleshly in us, what is earthly not heavenly: sexual immorality, impurity, passion, evil desire, covetousness, which is idolatry. God's wrath is coming upon people and the world because of these sins. We will escape because of our union with Christ, but we should live according to who we *are* in Him not who we *were*. We used to live for lust before we were united to Christ; now, we must live for Christ from our hearts, because He is our life, and we have left sin and death behind, have put on Christ, and are being conformed to His image.

We owe our lives to God not our lusts. Christ has freed us from the power of sin, and His Spirit empowers us to live for Him. We must sacrifice our fleshly desires, and instead, be transformed by the renewing of our minds through reading, receiving, and believing His word.

Application

When you lust, you show that your heart is not content with God or His good provisions. You're jealous of Him, so you're willing to twist His good creation, your own body and others, to fulfill your evil desires. But lust cannot satisfy you because you are God's image-bearer and He is conforming you to the image of His Son Jesus Christ. Yet, lust wants to conform you to mirror an unbeliever who is dead in sin, who you used to be, but are no longer.

When you lust, you show that you're focused on this temporary life not eternal life. You can't aim at Jesus in Heaven at God's right hand, and lust. God's wrath will come upon the world for sins like impurity and covetousness, but as those born again in Christ, we're too good for lust. You know and have experienced too much good, truth, and beauty in Christ, to lust, and you have even more waiting on you in eternity.

Today, will you be content with God's design, His provisions for you, and how He's governing all creation? Will you fix your eyes on Christ and Heaven in eternity, where you will be soon? Will you remind yourself that only God can satisfy you, and lust cannot? Will you pray often and hear, read, receive, and believe God's word? By the Spirit, you can put lust to death today, but will you?

Marching Orders: Thinking God's Thoughts After Him

Receive, believe, and live the truths you've read. Memorize and meditate on these truths today:

One Sentence to Shape Your Affections:

Since I am created in God's image and I'm being conformed to Christ's likeness, only God can satisfy me, not lust or any other sin.

One Poem to Shape Your Affections:

Lust whispers lies, a fleeting thrill to chase,
It sows discontentment with God's good will and grace.
It twists His gifts, it clouds my heart and mind,
It short sights my eyes to lose vision of heaven's kind.

Yet I, raised with Christ, am born anew,
Born again, I am God's child, one of the few.
My heart, once dead, now seeks His holy face,
To live with Him in everlasting grace.

From fleshly desires I turn and depart,
Thanksgiving heals the jealous Christian heart.
In worship, prayer, and the word I find,
A transformed life, a pure and renewed mind.

Christ has won, and I'm in Him,
While God's wrath comes for the world's sin.
No debt to lust, but to Jesus alone I owe,
A life of love, a rushing river to overflow.

So, fix your eyes on Christ enthroned above,
His beauty, His truth, His everlasting love.
Content in Him, my lust will fade and dim,
As I live for Heaven, forever united to Him.

One Song to Shape Your Affections:

Add this song to your playlist, "Gladly Would I Leave Behind Me."

On YouTube,
By Sovereign Grace Music (Written by Ann Griffiths, Doug Plank)

https://www.youtube.com/watch?v=qm4KGWvz4KU

1. Gladly would I leave behind me
All the pleasure I have known
To pursue surpassing treasures
At the throne of God the Son

Worthy of unending worship
Love and loveliness is He
By His precious death were millions
From the jaws of death set free[32]

[Due to copyright laws, I cannot include the rest of the lyrics here, but they are included in the above video.]

End with Prayer

---

[32] Ann Griffiths, "Gladly Would I Leave Behind Me," Accessed November 4, 2025, https://sovereigngracemusic.com/music/songs/gladly-would-i-leave-behind-me/.

Next Steps

After 33 days of applying the truths in this devotional, are you more sanctified now than before you read it? If you were full of lust when you started this devotional, how do you compare now? How much progress have you made?

No Progress

If you've not made any progress, you need to read this work again with a believing heart and apply its principles every day. You also need to spend more time in prayer, in God's word, and with Christians. You may need to get rid of the Internet or TV, or your cell phone, until you are strong enough in the Lord to have these things without them tempting you.

Some Progress

If you've made some progress, you need to read this work again, memorizing the shorter (page 217) and larger (223) catechisms, until you've mortified the lust in your heart completely. Also, to further think on the truth presented each day, write a poem to summarize what you've read or a poem of response.

Almost or Complete Progress

If you've developed new patterns of holy impulses, desires, thoughts, and actions, rejoice and keep exercising these habits.

If this devotional has helped you to be almost completely or completely free from lust, please share your copy with others so that they too can increase in their enjoyment of Christ and in their hatred for lust.

Freedom From Lust Shorter Catechism

1. Why does God's eternal nature surpass the temporary and fleeting nature of lust?

God is eternal, has no beginning, no end, no parts, no needs, and He exists in and of Himself from eternity past, now, and forever; while lust began in the serpent's heart, will end in the Lake of Fire, and only offers fleeting pleasure that quickly fades.

2. How does God's holiness expose the emptiness of lust?

God is beyond my full understanding and knows more and better than I do, yet He has revealed Himself to me through creation and the Bible, showing me His perfect goodness, which exposes lust as empty and unable to satisfy me.

3. How does God's sovereign power expose the weakness of lust?

God is Creator, doing whatever He pleases, accomplishing His holy will by giving His word, and giving and taking life for His own glory; while lust has no power over me unless I permit it.

4. How does God's complete knowledge reveal that lust leads only to destruction?

Only God knows all that has been, will be, could have been or could be, and He gave me some of His knowledge in the Bible, exactly what I need so that I will flourish; therefore, lust is and can only be the path to failure.

5. How does God's all-presence reveal the limited nature of lust?

God is independent from His creation, though He freely fills all time and space, and no one can hide from His presence or be ripped from His love in Christ; while lust is only present in sinners and will not exist in eternity with Jesus.

6. How does God's unlearned wisdom expose the folly of lust?

With no counsel, help, input from anyone, or learning, God wisely made and governs all things, while lust twists God's life-giving creation into sin and death.

7. How does God's justice demand accountability for lust through His word?

God, being inherently holy and just, has crafted His word in the same vein; thus, He holds everyone accountable to live in obedience to it from our hearts; therefore, those who lust will suffer loss, and if possible, death and hell.

8. How does God's truthfulness reveal lust as a lie from the devil?

God is true, and all that He does is true, and everything contrary to Him mirrors the devil, who is the father of lies; therefore, lust deceives, promising joy only to deliver suffering, sin, and death.

9. Why is lust ugly when compared to God and His design?

God is beauty and His design is beautiful; thus, all that is contrary to Him and His design is inherently ugly; therefore, lust is ugly and is the pursuit of ugliness.

10. How does God's love reveal that lust is hate?

God is love, His design reflects this love, and all those born of Him live in love, which means that all that is contrary to Him or His design is hate; therefore, lust hates God, His design, me and others.

11. Why does the selfless unity of the Trinity reveal that lust selfishly takes not gives?

There is one God who eternally exists in three distinct Persons: Father, Son, and Holy Spirit; the Father lovingly begets the Son; the Son is lovingly begotten from the Father; the Spirit lovingly proceeds from the Father and the Son; these three Persons are one Divine Nature; therefore, since lust is not from God, it does not give but selfishly takes of myself and others for sin.

12. How does God's unchanging nature expose lust's constant changing and broken promises?

God is unchanging, it's what He is; and He can never break His commitments, it's who He is, but lust always changes and can never satisfy me.

13. How does Jesus being the God Man, and Christians being conformed to His image, expose lust as mirroring Satan?

Jesus, truly God and truly Man, is united to two natures, union without mixture and distinction without separation, in His Divine Person; and all Christians are being conformed to His perfect image; while lust rebels against God, seeking to conform me to Satan's image.

14. How does Jesus' victory over the serpent encourage me to mortify my lust?

Jesus Christ came to crush the serpent's head, fulfilling the types and shadows of Adam and Noah; while lust seeks to repeat the lives of Cain and all those destroyed in the flood.

15. How does the prophets longing for Jesus, not lust, encourage me to mortify my lust?

Jesus Christ, the Seed of the woman, of Abraham, came to crush the serpent's head, fulfilling all the Old Testament types and shadows; while lust seeks to repeat the lives of all those who rejected YHWH in history.

16. How does Israel and David longing for Jesus, not lust, encourage me to mortify my lust?

Jesus Christ is the Seed of the woman, of Israel, of David, God's true Son, reigning on David's eternal throne forever; while lust is the seed of Satan, of the Canaanites, of the Philistines.

17. How does Jesus as the true Prophet call me to obey Him rather than lust?

Jesus, the eternal true Prophet prophesied by Moses, came to proclaim God's word to the world, while lust denies Jesus's words and morals.

18. How does Jesus' intercession as the true High Priest encourage me to go to Him rather than to lust?

Jesus Christ is the ultimate High Priest, the fulfillment of all the priests who came before Him, interceding with His own death and righteousness for both believing Jew and Gentile before God; while lust cannot stand in God's presence and harms my relationship with God.

19. How does Jesus' righteous rule as King of kings encourage me to submit to Him rather than lust?

Jesus, the King of kings and Son of David, rules in righteousness over all creation on David's throne forever, while lust seeks to dethrone Christ in my heart.

20. Why does Jesus' Lordship and salvation deliver me from the harm and deception of lust?

Jesus is Savior and Lord, the only way to be saved from my sins and reconciled to God; while lust seeks to condemn me and alienate me from God.

21. Why does the Holy Spirit's indwelling of Christians empower us to repent of lust?

The Holy Spirit is truly God, and by Him, the Father and Son live within all Christians, empowering me to turn from lust, turn to Christ, and kill the lust in my heart.

22. How does the Holy Spirit's sanctifying work transform me to love God, and to hate lust?

The Holy Spirit brings eternal life by regenerating me, sanctifying me, and empowering me to live out the fruit He is producing in my heart; while lust cuts me, injures me, and hinders my relationship with God.

23. How does the Holy Spirit enable me to overcome lust, which immerses me in sin and death?

John prepared the way for Christ to baptize His disciples with the Holy Spirit, as the prophet Joel foretold, who all Christians are immersed in through faith in Christ, while lust seeks to immerse me in sin and death.

24. How does dwelling on lust make me reflect Satan more than Christ?

My impulses, thoughts, actions, and patterns shape me for good or for ill: dwelling on God and His righteousness, transforms me into His image, but fixating on lust makes me reflect Satan.

25. How does lust devalue my body and other image-bearers created for God's glory?

My body was created for God's glory, not sexual immorality, so any lustful impulse, desire, thought, or action devalues both others and me as His image-bearers.

26. Why do tempters and pornography, as tools for lust, lead me toward spiritual death and separation from God?

Tempters and pornography are serial killers that stand in death and hell and will drag me there if possible.

27. How does lust pervert God's design for marriage and singleness?

God designed me as male or female for marriage, with singleness as the exception, to reflect His glory, not for lust.

28. How does lust hide God's glory and deny His wisdom?

When I use God's creation in a way that twists His design, like lust, I dishonor His glory, claiming my wisdom surpasses His.

29. How does Christ's beauty draw me to Him, and away from lust?

Christ, God the Son in the flesh, is the most beautiful of all creation, and sees me and draws me to love and enjoy Him above all things, for He is of infinite worth, and exposes lust as worthless.

30. How does my identity in Christ empower me to flee lust and to live for Him?

Christ is my identity; therefore, God calls me to flee lust and to live for Him, empowered by His Holy Spirit to live a redeemed life.

31. Who is responsible for my lust?

I am responsible for every evil impulse that springs up in my heart, including lust, and by the Holy Spirit's power within me, I can repent and pursue loving God with all my heart, soul, and mind.

32. How has God equipped me to grow in His virtues and repent of lust?

By His Spirit through Christ, God has saved me and empowered me to add and increase in His virtues, not lust, gradually maturing me in Christ until He completes in eternity what He started in me.

33. Why can lust never satisfy me?

Since I am created in God's image and I'm being conformed to Christ's likeness, only God can satisfy me, not lust or any other sin.

Freedom From Lust Larger Catechism

1. Why does God's eternal nature surpass the temporary and fleeting nature of lust?

God eternal, no start, no end,
No parts, no needs, we all on Him depend.
Past, now and forever, He simply is,
In Him, eternal bliss, my salvation begins.

But lust began in the serpent's heart,
And bids me, from God to depart.
Promising me bliss with a deathly kiss,
Its pleasures flee, as I hear the serpent hiss.

2. How does God's holiness expose the emptiness of lust?

God, beyond my grasp, yet finitely known,
The Creator, not of flesh and bone.
Yet through prophets, apostles, and Christ's grace,
In creation and Scripture, He reveals His face.

His wisdom vast, His insight pure,
He knows better and more than me, I am sure.
His righteousness revealed, all good is He,
In perfect holiness, His essence be.
But lust, my life, it soils,

And my relationship with God, it spoils.
Emptiness is its nature, and all it does bring,
Twists my senses deaf, I can't hear creation sing.

3. How does God's sovereign power expose the weakness of lust?

God, the almighty Creator,
Designer of all that's good.
Of sin alone, He is not the Maker,
His power is everywhere understood.

He acts with sovereign purpose, high and free,
Gives and takes by His decree.
His timeless word, true and bright,
Given in the Bible, His truth is light.

But lust needs my permission,
A cancer to grow without remission.
This parasite eats my heart into a crater,
Drinking my life away, as it mocks my Creator.

4. How does God's complete knowledge reveal that lust leads only to destruction?

God knows all that can be known,
Past and future, He alone.
Learning's not for Him, the Creator,
Master of all knowledge, none greater.

What does man know? A fleeting breath,
Here for a moment, and then death.
Without God's voice to light my way,
Lust and death await me each day.

But God, my beacon, hope, and guide,
In His knowledge I safely abide.
He knows what's best for mankind,
In Him, truth and love, I always find.

5. How does God's all-presence reveal the limited nature of lust?

God does not need what He has made,
For creation only exists in His shade.
He forever reigns outside His design,
Yet fills each moment, all of time.

No man can hide from God's infinite being,
His presence, His love, He is all-seeing.
He loves His church in Christ without end,
A bond that finite lust can never rend.

6. How does God's unlearned wisdom expose the folly of lust?

God's canvas vast, from glory done,
Each thread of creation, His wisdom spun.
Small I am, and vast is He,
Beyond His word, His wisdom, a mystery.

When I can't grasp at understanding,
It's my fault, not His planning.
No one can counsel His mind,
He is God, we are mankind.

No gift can I give to Him in return,
For all I know and am, from Him I learn.
My reason and quest to understand,
Are but gifts from His loving hand.

How dare I question my Creator's deeds,
When all that is good in me, from Him proceeds.
My reasoning, my thoughts, my very speech,
Are His gifts, yet if I lust, to Him I preach.

7. How does God's justice demand accountability for lust through His word?

Holy and just, my God stands supreme,
His law, His word, a glorious beam.
To display His nature, so pure so bright,
A perfect guide, both day and night.

Like Him, His word, a fountain of good,
Brings unlimited blessings, as only it could.
Just and holy, He calls me to be,
Mirroring His nature for all to see.

Fulfilled by Christ, the law and word,
Freeing me with His righteousness, like a bird.
He takes my lust, my heart of stone, away,
Gifts me His Spirit and a new heart, so I won't stray.

8. How does God's truthfulness reveal lust as a lie from the devil?

God is true, unchanging, light,
While men are liars, lost in night.
Lust sprouts from my heart of sin,
It comes from within, where lies begin.

Yet God, His nature, is firm and sure,
His truth endures, steadfast, pure.
Promises made, He will not break,

His love, even life and death cannot shake.

God sent His Son, Jesus Christ,
To teach me truth, to give me sight.
Through Him, God's truth I see,
And now in Christ, I see me.

"In Him who is true," I boldly stand,
In Jesus Christ, the Son of Man.
He is the true God, being life without end,
Himself He gives, my heart and soul to mend.

9. Why is lust ugly when compared to God and His design?

From Zion, the Savior comes, Jesus Divine,
God's Son Incarnate, Beauty's true design.
Perfection embodied, in Him beauty's peak,
A testament to the Creator, heard by the humble and meek.

Yet voices around me, they whisper and say,
"Beauty's in the beholder," in a subjective way.
But this view is fleeting, like shadows at noon,
For beauty, true beauty, is not mine to assume.

Solomon in wisdom, in Ecclesiastes he penned,
That beauty is timeless, from God's hand to send.
Not by the eye of man, but by Divine sight,
Beauty is fixed, from God's perfect light.

So let me see beauty as God does define,
Not through my lustful vision, but His flawless design.
For all that He creates, in time, comes to be,
A reflection of His beauty, for all eternity.

10. How does God's love reveal that lust is hate?

Before the cosmos, earth, and sea,
God was there, loving Himself supremely.
He is His own Beloved, eternally true,
Loving Himself from the ages through.

I've come to know Him, in His love,
A love and knowledge the world dreams of.
I trust in His love that He has freely shown,
The love that calls me to His throne.

The world will hate, my flesh does fight,
And lust may cloud my inner light.
But if I abide in love, with God I'll stay,
He in me, and I in Him, with Christ always.

11. Why does the selfless unity of the Trinity reveal that lust selfishly takes not gives?

From ancient days, the faithful knew,
The triune God, infinite, true.
One God alone, eternal, vast,
Three Persons distinct, the First and Last.

All that the Father is in light,
The Son and Spirit are by right.
Their distinction lies in order's trace,
Not in their being, but their logical place.

The Father begets the Son always,
Eternal birth in timeless days.
The Holy Spirit proceeds from Father and Son,
Distinct in order as these Three are One.

The Trinity in loving harmony, my selfish lusts to mend,
So, I will reflect Him without end.
From the Father, Son, and Spirit's throne,
Let selflessness and love in me be sown.

12. How does God's unchanging nature expose lust's constant changing and broken promises?

God, the unchanging One, forever whole,
Self-existent, sovereign, and in control.
No need He has, and no lack to find,
No change for better or worse, not even His mind.

His promises, true, His decrees are certain,
With no veil of deceit, and no shadowing curtain.
But lust deceives, and is ever changing,
Leading its followers to the end of a noose, hanging.

13. How does Jesus being the God Man, and Christians being conformed to His image, expose lust as mirroring Satan?

Jesus, YHWH the Son, with me dwells,
His way, paved by the Baptist, hear Isaiah's voice.
Sole Knower of the Father's boundless wells,
He shares that spring only by sovereign choice.

Man and God, one Divine Person in Mary's frame,
Holy-Spirit-wrought, the Word took breath,
Felt my thirst and hunger, and bore my shame,
Mirroring God through life, yet obedient to death.

Two Natures united in God the Son,
One truly human, one truly Divine,

Unmixed, yet distinct without separation,
Natures different, but no rift, no severing line.

Me, from Adam's seed but in Christ born again,
Predestined by the Father's will, in Christ to share.
Lustful humanity, chosen by God, never to sin,
To reflect Him, His holy likeness, forever to wear.

14. How does Jesus' victory over the serpent encourage me to mortify my lust?

In His image, God created man and wife,
To mirror His ways through mortal life.
Reflecting His morality, reason, love, and reign,
Yet sin stained all, spreading the serpent's fame.

But God spoke hope in Eden's dark shade,
The woman would give birth; the serpent would be slayed.
His heel pierced through, death would be His cost,
Legion would laugh, but redemption's hope would not be lost.

Man's evil swelled, till God's flood swept through,
Yet grace upheld Noah, Shem, and Japheth, faithful and true.
A new Adam stood, his kin on the ark aboard,
But sin still lurked in Ham's heart, he and the serpent in accord.

By God's design, from Shem's line, the Christ would spring,
The serpent's doom laid bare at the feet of salvation's King.
At Eden's lustful breach, a promise was given,
And from an angel I hear, "He is not here, for He has risen."

15. How does the prophets longing for Jesus, not lust, encourage me to mortify my lust?

God's image shines in mankind alone,
Not animal nor angel claims this throne.
From dust to Adam, a human tale,
True man chose sin, and all men fell.

A man brought death, a Man must save,
Only the woman's Seed, pure and brave.
Her offspring crushes the serpent's head,
Though bruised, He triumphs over the dead.

Through Abraham, the promise flows,
A single line where blessing grows.
Isaac born, then Jacob true,
In Judah's line, the King breaks through.

From Eden's Fall to Zion's Son,
One chosen Seed, the Holy One.
Abraham stumbles, David sins,
Yet their Son, my heart, He mends.

Trace the Seed with a steadfast gaze,
A thread of grace through a shadowed maze.
At last He comes, the woman's Seed,
Abraham's joy, the luster's need.

16. How does Israel and David longing for Jesus, not lust, encourage me to mortify my lust?

From Eden's curse, history would unfold,
Two lines of seed, as God foretold:
The serpent's brood, the woman's kin,

A war the Sinless One would win.

God's chosen people clash with rebel heart,
Noah and Shem, and Ham apart.
Abraham stood against the nations bold,
And Israel was born from prophecies of old.

Hosea's call in Matthew rings,
From Gentile land, the Son of God springs.
Fleeing Herod's cruel blade,
In Egypt's shade, His refuge was made.

From death's dark tomb, Christ rose, a King so grand,
To reign on David's throne by God's command.
God the Son, victory won, lust's crushing has begun,
Jesus to soon return, to bring His kingdom, under the Son.

17. How does Jesus as the true Prophet call me to obey Him rather than lust?

A prophet speaks God's word to men,
Moses lived that role back then.
Matthew unveils Christ the Prophet true,
Fulfilling what an elderly Moses knew.

Pharaoh's sword sought Moses' life,
Herod's rage brought Jesus strife.
Egypt hid them both from harm,
Saved by God's plan under Gentile arm.

Forty days, in the wilderness tried,
Yet, Jesus rejected the devil's pride.
Forty years, Israel roamed astray,

Tested and tempted in Moses' day.

Moses climbed to Sinai's height,
On that mount, the law brought to sight.
Jesus preached with power unfurled,
A forgotten law, explained to a waiting world.

Transfigured on a peak so grand,
Moses radiated by God's command.
Jesus shined, as if the sun's own kin,
From the cloud, God's voice exalted Him then.

Three men joined Moses, three too with Christ,
Clouds engulfed, and fear sufficed.
From the midst, God's voice rang clear,
"Listen to my Son! Prick up your ear!"

Moses longed for the woman's Seed, then Jesus came,
The True Prophet of endless fame.
God's beloved, the final call,
In Him, not lust, the prophets find their all.

18. How does Jesus' intercession as the true High Priest encourage me to go to Him rather than to lust?

God forgave through Levite rites, not their power,
The disabled, excluded from worship, unclean every hour.
Jesus, supreme High Priest, God's Son Divine,
Heals and forgives with power, His glory to shine.

God the Son on the Mount, taught with authority,
The law to fulfill, to set free from the Pharisee.
Priests marked the clean, the unclean set apart,

Jesus divided them by faith, discerning the heart.

Leprosy judged, priests marked the stain,
But Jesus cleansed the lepers, healing their pain.
Ahaz brought idols. Hezekiah and Levite, the temple renewed,
And Jesus cleansed the temple, a den of thieves subdued.

Pure, He cleansed what the lustful did defile,
He is the eternal High Priest, in Him is no guile.
Interceding for His people, His love remains and sustains,
Fulfilling all High Priests, with grace He forever reigns.

19. How does Jesus' righteous rule as King of kings encourage me to submit to Him rather than lust?

From David's line, as Nathan foretold,
His Son would shine, his throne to hold.
Jesus, in righteousness, would lead the way,
Freeing God's people from lust's dark sway.

Born of Mary, of Heli's sacred line,
Of Joseph's house, where lineages intertwine.
The angel said, Mary's womb would bring,
God's own Son, the everlasting King.

20. Why does Jesus' Lordship and salvation deliver me from the harm and deception of lust?

Jesus Christ, God's only Son,
Born to heal what lust had done.
Son of David, the promised King,
Hope to the world, His mercies bring.

Savior and Lord, no other Name,
Jesus, perfectly holy, forever the same.
He is the Way, the Truth, and the Life,
Saving from God's wrath, lust, and strife.

Lord and Christ, the Messiah true,
Fulfilling the word the prophets knew.
Bow to Him, both Lord and King,
Eternal Life, His love will bring.

21. Why does the Holy Spirit's indwelling of Christians empower us to repent of lust?

Holy Spirit, with Father and Son, eternal,
My Seed of salvation, my Kernel.
He is neither angel, nor fleeting force,
But God Himself, creation's Source.

Distinct, Divine, a Person true,
He speaks, He guides, His will to do.
Grieved by lust, yet interceding,
He glorifies Christ, His people, leading.

Not a mere power, but God Most High,
On His mind and voice, the saints rely.
Sent by Jesus, from His Father's throne,
He dwells in me, I'm never alone.

Three yet One, in unity bound,
Father, Son, in Holy Spirit found.
Receiving the Spirit, Three Persons I gain,
God's love within me, forever to reign.

22. How does the Holy Spirit's sanctifying work transform me to love God, and to hate lust?

In Ezekiel, a new covenant, God's promise foretold,
A new heart, a new Spirit, on the same old road.
My heart from stone to flesh, God's Spirit within,
Empowers me to walk in Him, not imputing sin.

Born again, from above, as Jesus decreed,
By Spirit and water, from lust I am freed.
No longer in Adam, but united to Christ's name,
The Spirit regenerates, ignites me in holy flame.

He indwells me, with the Father and Son,
In Christ we're united, our hearts becoming one.
Washed, justified, and sanctified, by His hand,
Declared righteous in Him, on His promise I stand.

No longer in the flesh, but alive in the Spirit,
Crucified with Christ, His life I inherit.
Love, joy, and peace, His fruit I now bear,
Walking with the Spirit till His glory, I share.

23. How does the Holy Spirit enable me to overcome lust, which immerses me in sin and death?

John the Baptist cleared the path,
For YHWH's Son, he preached with wrath.
"Repent, bear fruit!" his cry rang true,
Before he'd baptize, a heart must be new.

Christ baptizes with His Spirit to flame,
To raise the spiritually dead, to guide, to claim.
Jesus promised, though He'd depart,

The Spirit's power would fill each believing heart.

In the upper room, the disciples prayed,
The Spirit came, their fears, He slayed.
Languages aflame, a rushing wind,
God's mighty work, their voices to send.

From every nation, Jews drew near,
God's word, in their languages, to hear.
Some scoffed, "They're drunk!" but Peter did cry,
"It's too early for new wine, hear Joel prophesy."

Paul declared, in Christ we rise,
The Spirit dwells where faith abides.
Though once dead in lust and flesh, Christ I gain,
By the Father's hand, I walk in the Spirit's reign.

24. How does dwelling on lust make me reflect Satan more than Christ?

I become like what I think on,
Idols I chase, or God's own Son.
From prison, Paul tells me to dwell,
On good, truth, beauty, not what leads to hell.

In Christ, Paul thrived in prosperity or pain,
For to him, to live was Christ, and death was gain.
James warns: If lust in my heart takes root,
It spawns mindful sin, death's bitter fruit.

All that's good flows from God's perfect throne,
But evil has a source and path all its own.
Choose the soil where righteousness will bloom,
Or cling to lust and reap sin's barren tomb.

25. How does lust devalue my body and other image-bearers created for God's glory?

By God, in the womb, I'm fearfully made,
His image displayed, His plans arrayed.
Before my breath, He wove my embryo,
Designed my days, my heart, my soul.

Not for lust was my body formed,
But for the Lord, by love transformed.
United to Christ, I'm not my own,
Yet my lust lures me, and seeds are sown.

Lust twists God's beauty, blinds my eye,
Sees not His glory but embraces a lie.
It hides His image, cloaks its light,
And aims at a false god of blackest night.

God's will be clear: I must reflect His light,
And see males and females with holy sight.
Lust defies His will, distorts His plan,
And robs my soul of what it is to be man.

26. Why do tempters and pornography, as tools for lust, lead me toward spiritual death and separation from God?

Smooth words weave a deadly spell,
Enticing hearts to death and hell.
In graves they stand, immodest, bold,
Luring souls to chains untold.

Serial killers stalking in the night,
Adulterers slay with fake delight.
None return from her embrace,

238

Lost forever away from Christ's face.

Yet deeper still, the tempter lives within,
My heart seduces me with lust and sin.
Christ's call is clear, severe, and true:
"Cut off your hand that tempts you."

Let no eye wander, nor touch betray,
Lest death and hell claim me as prey.
With millstone weight, the tempter is doomed,
If I repent, reject, I'll see them entombed.

27. How does lust pervert God's design for marriage and singleness?

From Adam's rib, God formed his bride,
A piece of him, no longer in his side.
From his rib removed, Eve came to be,
Both incomplete, longing for their unity.

God joined them together, one flesh to form,
A man leaves his kin, and to his wife is sworn.
In every soul, this truth is spun,
Male and female, created to be one.

Yet Paul praised singleness, a gift rare,
For some to serve God, free from worldly care.
But marriage sings of God's great plan,
His church united in Christ, by the Spirit's hand.

From Jesus' side, blood and water flowed free,
His Spirit given to me, reborn to be.
As Eve from Adam, the church from Christ,
Not for lust, but one flesh through His sacrifice.

28. How does lust hide God's glory and deny His wisdom?

Satan mocked Job's worship, not in part,
Said God's blessings alone won his heart.
He sneered, "Job's faith is all for naught,
Strip your gifts, he'll curse You; he's bought."
Not just Job, but God he dared to scorn,
"God's worthy only when His gifts adorn."

Solomon taught, cling to wisdom's hand,
A sister to guide through treacherous land.
For the temptress seduces with honeyed lies,
With "love" and "delight" where every fool dies.
Immature men lust beneath twilight's shade,
Thinking sin's price will never be paid.

Lust twists God's design, in Satan's guile,
Saying, "I'll use God's creation to self-defile."
It scorns God's plan, claiming wiser ways,
Spurning His gifts, mocking Him who saves.
Yet wisdom cries, "Flee the temptress, desire what's right,
Seek life through Christ or dig your grave tonight."

29. How does Christ's beauty draw me to Him, and away from lust?

Peter vowed to stand, faithful to the end,
Yet denied Christ thrice, submitting to sin.
Trusting himself, not Jesus, he lied with haste,
"I do not know Him," each with more distaste.

First to a servant, then with an oath profane,
Using God's name in vain, a more heinous stain.
An hour later, curses extended his shame,
But Christ pierced the dark, sparking holy flame.

How could he deny such perfect love?
His heart turned, and tears fell like a dove.
"Feed My lambs, tend My sheep," hear Christ call,
Love Him in heart, soul, and mind, stand tall.

See Christ gaze, weep and run to His side,
Where infinite love and blessings abide.
For lust trades Beauty for blight,
But repentance trades darkness for Light.

30. How does my identity in Christ empower me to flee lust and to live for Him?

Strive for holiness, Christ's chosen kin,
Like Paul, do not let complacency win.
Set apart from lust, the world's dark sway,
Control your body, desire faith's bright way.

Fear God's discipline, though it's His love's embrace,
For His correction comes to eliminate sin's every trace.
In Christ, heaven's sure, but rewards may suffer loss,
Live pure in heart and deed, like Jesus, not dross.

Run from youth's passions, as Timothy did learn,
Pursue righteousness and peace, where love's fires burn.
Sober mind, leave old sins behind, once your shame,
Now, baptized in the Name, and not your own fame.

Fear God not man, and not the mirror,
For your identity is Christ, so see Him clearer.
Called not to impurity, but holy obscurity,
The blood of Jesus, your all, your only surety.

31. Who is responsible for my lust?

In Eden's lush beauty, Eve denied her duty,
Through serpent eyes, she called evil, beauty.
She coveted as wise what God forbade,
Her lust took root, her heart betrayed.

No spark of lust is free from guilt,
Root and fruit require my blood to be spilt.
God's trials mature me, but never entice,
My lust alone breeds sin's dark vice.

I tempt myself, my heart deceives,
I lay with the devil, and sin conceives.
Unrepentance feeds lust until it grows to death,
A leech sucking precious years of fleeting breath.

Repent of lust at the root, confess the sin,
Turn to Christ, His grace will win.
Mourn your lust, trade joy for pain,
Humble yourself, God's mercy is gain.

Adulterous hearts chase worldly lust,
Their prayers falter, they're enthralled by dust.
Submit to God, and resist the foe,
Draw near to Him, and His commands will sow.

Before lust consumes, pursue what's right,
A godly spouse, a covenant bright.
Flee from sin, embrace God's call,
Repent, rejoice, and pursue Christ, your all.

32. How has God equipped me to grow in His virtues and repent of lust?

From God flows all good, truth, and beauty,
He sends His Spirit to produce life and duty.
He unites us to Christ, His glory to show,
By grace, His word, our hearts truly know.

No god am I, yet a partaker of His Nature Divine,
United to the God Man, as a branch to the Vine.
He gives me a new heart; in Him I'm born again,
Idols torn, by the Spirit's power, I'm freed from sin.

Increase in faith, add virtue, then knowledge seek,
To Self-control, add perseverance, aim at the Peak.
Add godliness, brotherly affection, and love abounding,
These guard my heart from Satan's relentless hounding.

Lacking these qualities, I'm blind, I fall,
Quickly forgetting Christ's work, who paid it all.
But increasing in these virtues, firm I'll stand,
Held fast within God's sovereign hand.

But if lust clouds my mind, my witness will fade,
Sin causes love for God and others to degrade.
Turn, repent, pursue the Spirit's fruit,
Put your sin to death, kill its root.

By grace, these virtues I must pursue,
Take responsibility, embrace what's true.
In Christ, I can stand, effective, free,
For God's glory, not my own, eternally.

33. Why can lust never satisfy me?

Lust whispers lies, a fleeting thrill to chase,
It sows discontentment with God's good will and grace.
It twists His gifts, it clouds my heart and mind,
It short sights my eyes to lose vision of heaven's kind.

Yet I, raised with Christ, am born anew,
Born again, I am God's child, one of the few.
My heart, once dead, now seeks His holy face,
To live with Him in everlasting grace.

From fleshly desires I turn and depart,
Thanksgiving heals the jealous Christian heart.
In worship, prayer, and the word I find,
A transformed life, a pure and renewed mind.

Christ has won, and I'm in Him,
While God's wrath comes for the world's sin.
No debt to lust, but to Jesus alone I owe,
A life of love, a rushing river to overflow.

So, fix your eyes on Christ enthroned above,
His beauty, His truth, His everlasting love.
Content in Him, my lust will fade and dim,
As I live for Heaven, forever united to Him.

Other Books by Dr. Jared Moore

1. You can read my articles and books as I write them, weekly, at my Substack[33] or Patreon[34] at "Dr. Jared Moore."

2. *The Lust of the Flesh: Thinking Biblically About "Sexual Orientation," Attraction, and Temptation.* Published by Free Grace Press.

3. *Same-Sex Attraction and the Temptation of Christ.* Published by Founders.

4. Co-author of *The Pop Culture Parent: Helping Kids Engage Their World for Christ.* Published by New Growth Press.

5. *A Biblical and Historical Appraisal of Concupiscence with Special Attention to Same-Sex Attraction.* Published by Southern Baptist Theological Seminary.

---

[33] https://drjaredmoore.com/.
[34] https://www.patreon.com/c/u16977519.

www.ingramcontent.com/pod-product-compliance
Lightning Source LLC
Chambersburg PA
CBHW051819090426
42736CB00011B/1561